W9-CEO-973

USBORNE COMPUTER GUIDES

COMPUTER GRAPHICS
& ANIMATION

Asha Kalbag

Designed by Russell Punter

Assistant designers: Michael Wheatley and Zöe Wray
Managing designer: Stephen Wright
Cover design by Isaac Quaye

Technical consultants: Merrick Brewer, Liam Devany, Michael Harvey,
Prof. Bob Stone, Andy Welch Ph.D.
Additional consultancy by Marc Carey

Illustrations by Russell Punter, Michael Wheatley and Merrick Brewer
Photography by Howard Allman
Edited by Philippa Wingate and Jane Chisholm
American editor: Carrie A. Seay

Computer graphics

What are computer graphics?

Computer graphics are pictures that have been created or changed on a computer. Computer graphics are used in a multitude of different areas, including architecture advertising, medicine and the movies.

Here are a few of the different things that can be produced with computer graphics.

Funny faces

Scenery for computer games

Designs for buildings

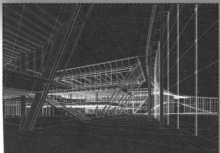

About this book

Computer Graphics & Animation starts by showing you how to create a variety of different pictures on your computer. You'll discover how to draw pictures from scratch, alter photographs and create your own animations.

As you produce your own computer graphics, you'll find out how your computer stores and displays them. You'll also find out what to do with your graphics once you've created them. There's advice on how to save them, print them out, and include them in other computer documents.

The book goes on to demonstrate how computer graphics experts use powerful computers and sophisticated software to produce exciting graphics for use in cartoons, computer games and films.

What do you need?

To create computer graphics, you will need a computer and some graphics software. There are different graphics programs for creating different kinds of pictures.

If you have a PC controlled by the Microsoft® Windows® operating system, you will already have a basic program for painting pictures on your screen. In Windows® 95 and 98, it is called Paint and in Windows® 3.1 it is called Paintbrush. If you have a Mac, you will need to obtain a basic painting program (see page 70).

To use your computer to alter photographs or create animations, you will need extra software. Turn to page 70 for information on how to find a variety of graphics software.

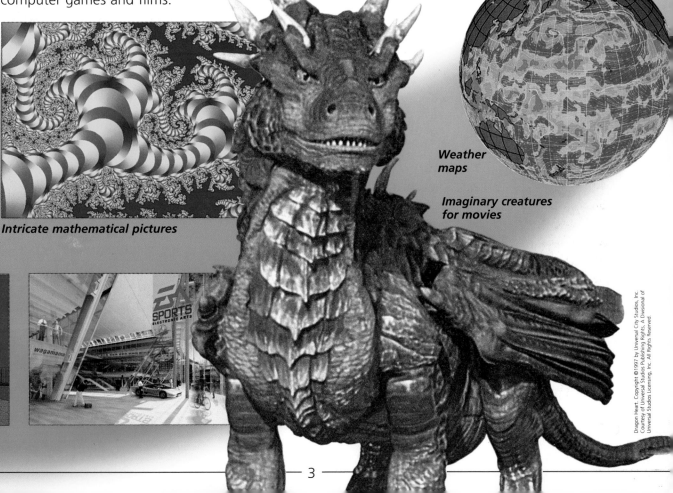

Intricate mathematical pictures

Weather maps

Imaginary creatures for movies

Painting pictures on screen

The simplest kind of graphics program is a painting program. This lets you create your own graphics from scratch. You can learn many essential computer graphics techniques by experimenting with a program like this.

About painting programs

One popular painting program is Paint, which comes free with the Microsoft® Windows® 95 and 98 operating systems.

Paint's window contains an area where you paint pictures, a color palette and a tool box. A tool box is a collection of buttons decorated with small pictures that represent drawing and painting tools.

Changing colors

Before you start painting, you need to select a color to draw on, known as a background color, and a color to draw with, called a foreground color.

You can change the background color by clicking on a color from the color palette with your right mouse button. To change the foreground color, click on a color with your left mouse button. The overlapping squares on the left of the color palette will display your selected foreground and background colors.

Foreground color

Background color

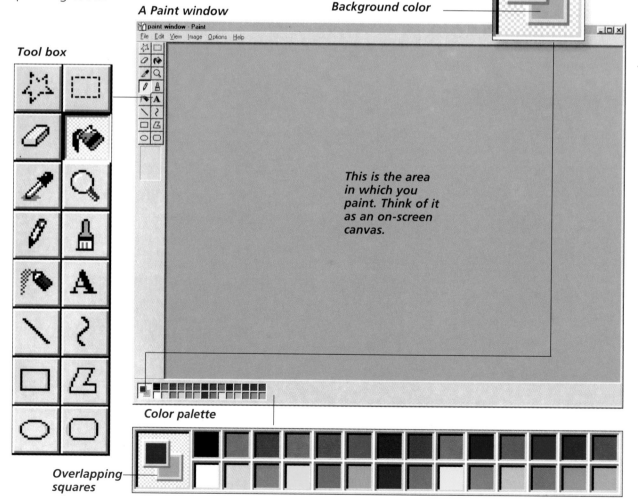

A Paint window

Tool box

This is the area in which you paint. Think of it as an on-screen canvas.

Color palette

Overlapping squares

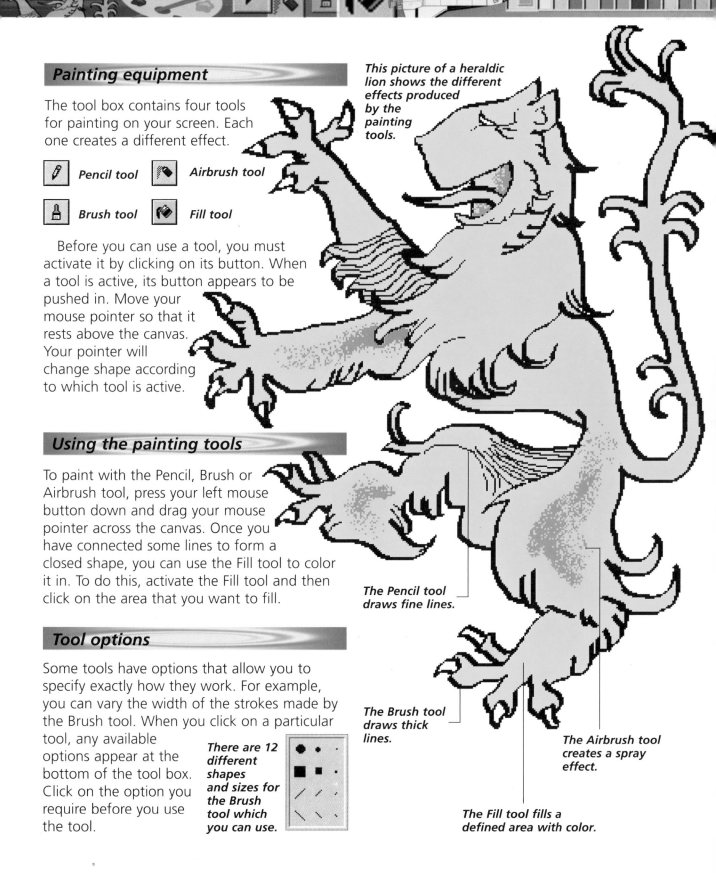

Painting equipment

The tool box contains four tools for painting on your screen. Each one creates a different effect.

Pencil tool

Airbrush tool

Brush tool

Fill tool

Before you can use a tool, you must activate it by clicking on its button. When a tool is active, its button appears to be pushed in. Move your mouse pointer so that it rests above the canvas. Your pointer will change shape according to which tool is active.

Using the painting tools

To paint with the Pencil, Brush or Airbrush tool, press your left mouse button down and drag your mouse pointer across the canvas. Once you have connected some lines to form a closed shape, you can use the Fill tool to color it in. To do this, activate the Fill tool and then click on the area that you want to fill.

Tool options

Some tools have options that allow you to specify exactly how they work. For example, you can vary the width of the strokes made by the Brush tool. When you click on a particular tool, any available options appear at the bottom of the tool box. Click on the option you require before you use the tool.

There are 12 different shapes and sizes for the Brush tool which you can use.

This picture of a heraldic lion shows the different effects produced by the painting tools.

The Pencil tool draws fine lines.

The Brush tool draws thick lines.

The Airbrush tool creates a spray effect.

The Fill tool fills a defined area with color.

Useful tools

Paint includes tools that give you more control over the things you draw, such as tools for drawing straight lines and rectangles. Many other graphics programs have similar tools.

Line tools

Paint has two tools that allow you to control the lines you draw.

Line tool

Curve tool

This picture is made from straight and curved lines.

To draw a straight line, click on the Line tool and move your mouse pointer to where you want the line to begin. Press the left mouse button down and drag your mouse. You can restrict the tool to creating vertical or horizontal lines, or lines at a 45° angle, by holding down the Shift key as you draw.

To create a curved line, click on the Curve tool and draw a straight line. You can then create curves by clicking at two points on it and dragging the line in different directions.

Shape tools

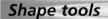

There are four tools that enable you to draw different shapes. To use a shape tool, click on its button, then move your mouse pointer to where you want the shape to appear. Press the left mouse button down and drag the mouse to create a shape.

Rectangle tool   **Polygon tool**

Ellipse tool   **Rounded Rectangle tool**

You can use the Rectangle and Ellipse tools to create perfect squares and circles by holding down the Shift key while you drag a shape.

The Polygon tool allows you to create shapes with many sides. Draw a line by dragging your mouse, then release your mouse button to change direction. Join the last line to the first line to close the shape.

Shading options

The shapes that you draw in Paint can be shaded in three different ways. When you activate a shape tool, the shading options will appear at the bottom of the tool box.

Below you can see the effects of the different shading options.

Shading options

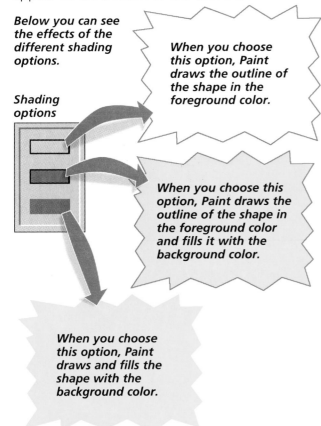

When you choose this option, Paint draws the outline of the shape in the foreground color.

When you choose this option, Paint draws the outline of the shape in the foreground color and fills it with the background color.

When you choose this option, Paint draws and fills the shape with the background color.

Picking a color

Most graphics programs have a tool which enables you to copy a color from anywhere in a picture for use elsewhere in the picture. In Paint, this is called the Pick Color tool.

To copy a color, first click on the Pick Color tool button, then click the part of the picture from which you want to copy the color. Click with your left mouse button to select the color as a foreground color or your right mouse button to select it as a background color.

Pick Color tool

Seeing close up

The Magnifier tool enables you to see an enlarged version of part of your picture. When you click on this tool, a rectangle will appear. Position it over the area that you want to magnify, and click with the left mouse button. You will see a close-up of that area. To see your picture at normal size again, activate the Magnifier tool again and click anywhere on your canvas.

Magnifier tool

Covering up mistakes

If you make a mistake, drag the Eraser tool over the part of your picture that you want to remove. It will cover this area with the currently selected background color.

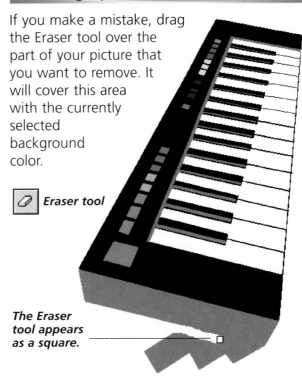

Eraser tool

The Eraser tool appears as a square.

Undoing and repeating

In most graphics programs, you can undo the last change you made to a picture by clicking on *Undo* on the *Edit* menu. If you preferred your picture before you undid something, select *Repeat* or *Redo* from the *Edit* menu. This will redo the alteration.

Graphics programs allow you to move, copy, delete or distort any part of a picture. First you need to indicate or "select" the area you want to alter. A selected area is called a selection.

Using a selection tool

Paint has two tools for selecting part of a picture: the Rectangle Selection tool and the Free-Form Selection tool.

 Rectangle Selection tool

 Free-Form Selection tool

To select a rectangular area, click on the Rectangle Selection tool button and drag a box over the area you wish to select. A broken line indicating your selection will appear. This line is called a marquee.

To deselect a selection, click with your mouse outside the marquee.

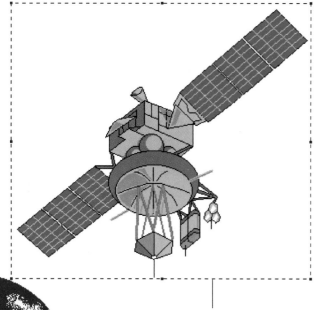

Marquee

A rectangular area containing the satellite has been selected in this picture.

Selecting other shapes

To select an area that isn't rectangular, you can use the Free-Form Selection tool. Click on the tool, then hold down your left mouse button and draw around the area that you want to select. A solid line will outline this area. When you connect the outline and release the mouse button, a rectangular marquee will replace the outline. Although your computer displays a rectangle, it registers the area outlined by the solid line as your selection.

Selecting an irregular shape with the Free-Form Selection tool

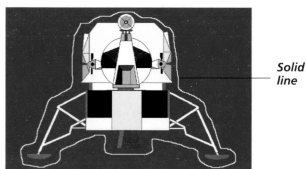

Solid line

A spacecraft shape has been selected.

Marquee

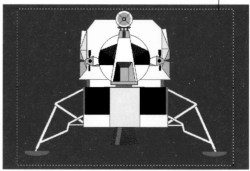

The program displays a rectangular marquee around the spacecraft shape.

Only the spacecraft shape is selected.

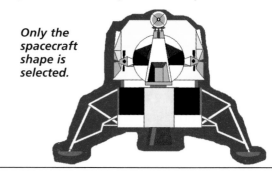

Selection options

You can use either selection tool to make two different kinds of selections: opaque selections and transparent selections. An opaque selection includes the background color of the selected area. A transparent selection contains only the foreground colors. When you click on a selection tool button, two pictures representing the selection options appear at the bottom of the tool box. Before you use the tool, click on the picture for the option you require.

These pictures show the different selection options.

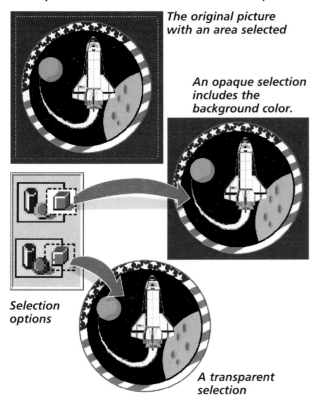

The original picture with an area selected

An opaque selection includes the background color.

Selection options

A transparent selection

Moving a selection

When you have made a selection, the mouse pointer changes to this shape: This indicates that you can move the selection around the canvas. To do this, hold down the left mouse button and drag the selection to a new location. You can move it as many times as you like while it remains selected.

These pictures show the different results obtained by moving a transparent selection and an opaque selection.

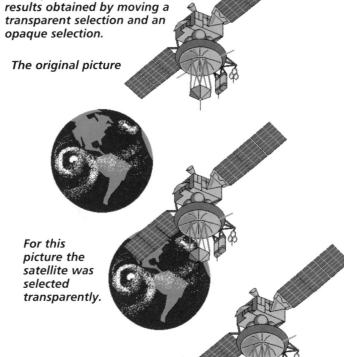

The original picture

For this picture the satellite was selected transparently.

For this picture the satellite was selected opaquely.

Deleting

To remove a selection from your picture, press the Delete key or choose the *Clear Selection* command from the *Edit* menu. The selection will be replaced by the currently selected background color.

Moving and copying

You can make a copy of a selection. To do this, hold down the Control key at the same time as you drag the selection. This leaves the original selection in place, but allows you to move a copy of it to a new location.

Cutting and pasting

Removing part of a picture and adding it to another picture is known as cutting and pasting.

Cutting

To cut out a part of your picture, select it and then choose *Cut* from the *Edit* menu. The selection will disappear from the picture and be replaced by the currently selected background color. The program does not delete the selection but, instead, stores it in a part of your computer's memory called the Clipboard.

Cutting a selection from a picture

The original picture

An area containing the CD was selected.

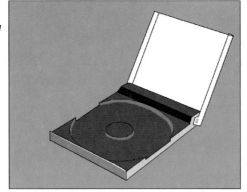

The picture with the selection removed

⚠ The Clipboard can only store one section of a picture at a time. Whenever you cut out a part of a picture, this replaces whatever was on the Clipboard before.

Pasting

Open the picture onto which you want to paste the cut-out section and choose *Paste* from the *Edit* menu. The cut-out section will appear in the second picture. You can also paste a selection onto a blank canvas.

The selection is pasted into the top left corner of the picture.

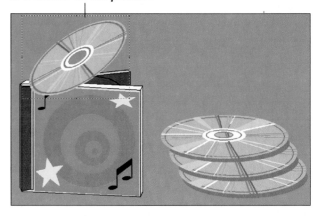

You can drag it to another location with your mouse.

Copying

You may wish to paste a selection from one picture into another without removing the selection from the first picture. To do this, go to the *Edit* menu and click on *Copy*. A copy of the selection will be stored on the Clipboard. You can paste this into another picture using the method described above.

Transforming your pictures

Graphics programs contain commands that allow you to transform a picture. For example, you can distort your picture, turn it around, or change its colors. You can apply these commands to the whole picture, or just to a selected area.

Giving instructions

To transform a picture in Paint, choose a command from the *Image* menu. When you select certain options, a box called a dialog box will appear on the screen. You complete this box to give a program precise instructions for carrying out a particular task.

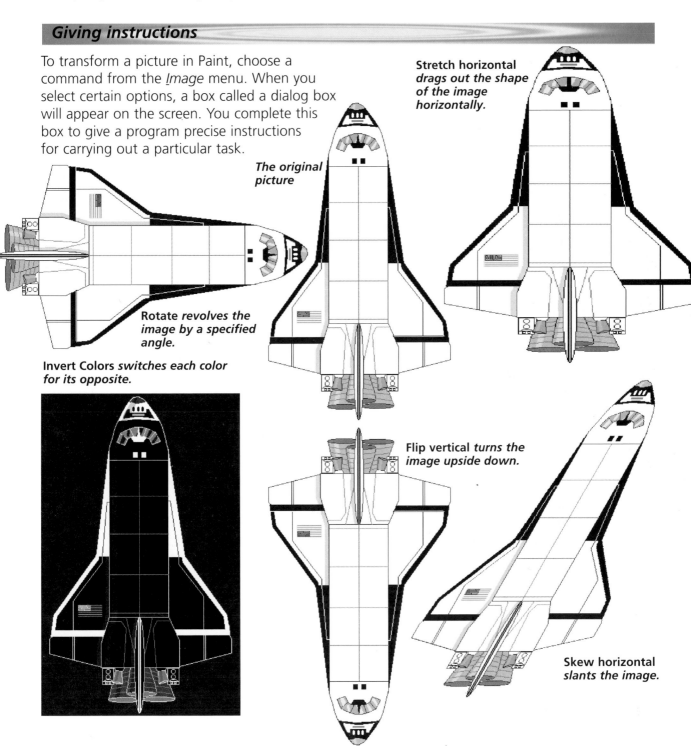

Stretch horizontal *drags out the shape of the image horizontally.*

The original picture

Rotate *revolves the image by a specified angle.*

Invert Colors *switches each color for its opposite.*

Flip vertical *turns the image upside down.*

Skew horizontal *slants the image.*

Using colors

You can add any color you like to a graphics program's color palette.

Ready-mixed colors

Each time you start Paint, the palette contains the same 28 colors. This is Paint's automatic selection from 48 colors which are called its Basic colors.

You will find the Basic colors in the Edit Colors dialog box. To open this dialog box, go to the *Options* menu and click on *Edit Colors...*

Paint's Basic colors

Paint's palette

Personalizing the palette

You can replace the colors in the palette with your own choice from the Basic colors. To do this, first select a color in the palette that you don't require with your left mouse button. Open the Edit Colors dialog box and click on a Basic color that you prefer. When you click *OK*, the second color will replace the first one in the palette.

This color palette contains greens, blues and grays. It was specially selected for painting pictures of underwater scenes.

Mixing paint

You can also create your own colors to add to the palette. To do this, choose a color to replace and open the Edit Colors dialog box as before. Next, click on the *Define Custom Colors>>* button to reveal another part of the dialog box. You will see a square that contains a rainbow of different colors. It is called the color matrix.

Paint's Edit Colors dialog box

Color matrix

This box shows the color that is currently selected.

Slider bar

Drag your pointer over the color matrix until the color you require appears in the Color/Solid box below. You can use the slider bar on the right to mix more white or black with your color. To add your color to the palette, click *Add to Custom Colors* and *OK*.

The Color/Solid box may contain two sections. This means your monitor is set to show 256 colors or less (see page 68). The left half shows you how much black or white the shade you have selected contains. The right half shows the color without any black or white added.

Red, green and blue

As you drag your pointer around the color matrix, the numbers in the boxes or "fields" underneath it change. The three fields on the right of the dialog box show the amounts of red, green and blue that make up a particular color. Try typing in new numbers (from 0 to 255) to see what color a particular combination of red, green and blue produces.

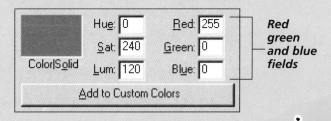

A section of the Edit Colors dialog box

Red green and blue fields

Color models

People, such as graphic designers, who work with colors on a computer screen, often describe them by the amounts of red, green and blue they contain. This method of describing a color is known as the RGB color model (R for red, G for green and B for blue).

A color model is a method that uses numbers to describe colors precisely. It allows people to distinguish between thousands of different colors. You can find out about another color model on page 30.

The colors of these seahorses have been described by the RGB model.

R0 G0 B255

R255 G255 B0

R128 G0 B128

R255 G0 B255

R0 G128 B128

R255 G0 B0

Saving colors

When you have made up a palette for a picture, you have to save it in order to use it for future pictures. To do this, choose *Save Colors...* from the *Options* menu. The Save Colors dialog box will appear on your screen. Give your palette a name and instruct your computer where to save it. You may want to create a new directory or folder for storing your palettes.

If you want to replace Paint's usual palette with a palette you have already created, click on *Get Colors...* on the *Options* menu. Use the dialog box to locate the palette you require. Highlight its name and click *OK*.

Paint's Save Colors dialog box

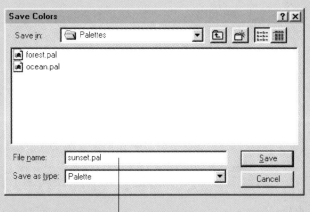

Paint saves palettes as .pal files.

Computers store all information, including pictures, as numbers. In this section you can find out about one of the methods that computers use to turn pictures into numbers.

Squares on a grid

A computer can store a picture as numbers by dividing it into a grid of tiny squares, known as picture elements or pixels. For each pixel, a computer records numbers that specify its location on the grid and its color.

Pictures that are turned into numbers using this method are known as raster or bitmap images. This is because the grid is called a raster or bitmap.

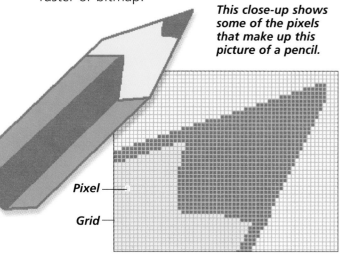

This close-up shows some of the pixels that make up this picture of a pencil.

Pixel

Grid

Seeing pixels

You can see how a raster image is divided into pixels by magnifying it. To do this in Paint, first draw a picture on the canvas, then choose *Zoom* from the *View* menu. From the menu that opens, click on *Large Size.* You will see a close-up of your picture. (If your picture doesn't fill the canvas, you may need to use the scroll bars to see it.) Once you have magnified a picture, you can see how it is made up of pixels on a grid, by choosing *View, Zoom* and then *Show Grid.*

Bits and bytes

Information that has been turned into numbers by a computer is called data. It is measured in units called bits and bytes. A bit is the smallest unit of data. Eight bits are called a byte and a kilobyte (KB) is just over 1,000 bytes.

When you save some computer data onto your computer's hard disk or another storage device, you create a collection of data called a file. The number of bytes of data in a particular file is known as its size. The more pixels a picture contains, the greater the number of bytes required to describe it. So pictures that contain more pixels produce bigger files.

A picture and a part of a picture that have been saved as separate files

The size of the file for this picture is 124 KB.

The size of the file for this part is only 29 KB.

Raster file formats

A computer can use different methods to arrange the data that makes up a file on disk. Each method is known as a file format.

The file format used by Paint is called Microsoft bitmap. Any picture saved as a Microsoft bitmap will have the file extension **.bmp**. (Find out about other formats used to store raster images on pages 23, 32-33 and 35.)

How many colors?

At least one bit of computer data is needed to record each pixel in a bitmap. The number of bits that a computer uses to store a pixel is known as bit depth.

When a computer saves a black and white picture, it uses only one bit per pixel. The higher the bit depth of a picture, the greater the range of colors a picture can contain. For example, a picture that uses 24 bits to record each pixel can contain up to 16.7 million different colors.

Saving pictures

To save a picture in Paint, click on *Save* on the *File* menu to call up the Save As dialog box. Give your picture a name and choose a location for it.

The *Save as type* section contains a drop-down list of types of Microsoft bitmap: monochrome, 16 color, 256 color or 24-bit bitmaps. These names refer to the maximum number of colors a picture can contain. Select the type of file you want to create from the list (see below), then click *OK*.

Below you can see the effects of saving a Microsoft bitmap in three different ways.

This is a 256 color version of the picture. It can contain up to 256 different colors. It requires 8 bits to record each pixel. The size of this file is 100 KB.

Swatara MS
1101 Highland Street
erlin-Steelton, PA 17113

This is a 16 color bitmap. It can contain up to 16 colors and requires 4 bits to describe each pixel. The size of this file is 40 KB.

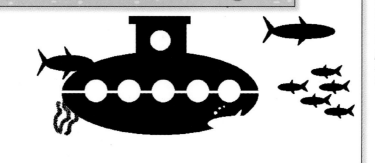

This is a monochrome (black and white) bitmap. It is a 1-bit picture. The size of this file is 10 KB.

Pictures from objects

Some graphics programs, known as drawing programs, create pictures that are built up from separate objects, such as lines and shapes, rather than individual pixels on a grid. Graphics made from objects are called object-oriented graphics or vector graphics (see below).

Drawing programs

Three popular drawing programs are Adobe® Illustrator®, CorelDRAW™ and Macromedia Freehand. These are all used by professional computer artists. A less expensive drawing program is Mayura Draw.

Paths and points

Every object created in a drawing program has an extra outline called a path. A path can consist of one or more lines. The end of each line is marked by a point.

These two pictures show objects and their paths.

Point   **Path**   **Point**

Point   **Point**

Path

A path for a straight line has two points.

A path for a triangle has three points.

Point

A drawing program records the position of the points and path that form each object as mathematical formulae, known as vectors. For this reason, object-oriented graphics are also known as vector graphics. A drawing program uses the vectors to calculate which parts of the screen need to be colored in order to produce the image.

Whole objects

A drawing program considers each line or shape in a picture to be a single, complete object. This makes it easy to make selections (see page 8).

To select a line or shape, simply click anywhere on it with the program's selection tool. You don't have to draw around the shape. This means that even fine lines or spirals and stars, like the ones on the right, can be selected simply by clicking on them.

Star

Octagon

Spiral

Independent objects

As each object in a vector graphic is separate and independent, you can change or remove a line or a shape without affecting other objects that make up the picture. For example, if you draw a frog on top of a lily pad and then remove the frog, the lily pad is unchanged.

A picture drawn in a drawing program

You can move and rotate the frog without changing the lily pad.

When you try the same thing with a raster graphic, part of the lily pad is removed as well.

Changing shape

To turn one shape into another shape, you need to add or remove points on its path. For example, by removing two of the points on an octagon's path, you create a path with six sides that produces a hexagon.

To turn the hexagon back into an octagon, you add two points to its path and then drag them to create a new shape.

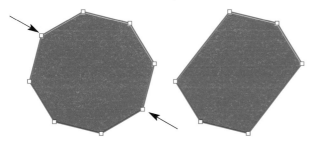

If you remove these two points, you will create the shape on the right.

Jagged edges

One advantage of vector graphics is that, when you make them bigger, diagonal lines and curves remain smooth. When you enlarge a raster graphic (see page 14), diagonal lines or curves will look jagged. This problem is known as aliasing or "the jaggies".

These two circles have been enlarged to twice their original size before printing.

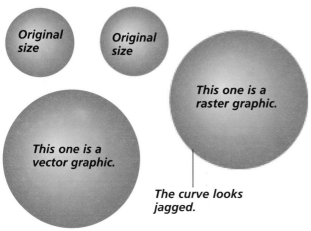

Original size

Original size

This one is a raster graphic.

This one is a vector graphic.

The curve looks jagged.

Creating curves

To produce a line, a drawing program needs to know the position of its start and end points. For a straight line, these are the only points it requires. For a curved line it needs two extra points which are not on the line. They are known as control points, because they determine the shape of a curve.

To create a curve, you position the start and end points and the control points. The computer calculates and draws the shape of the curve.

Curves that are produced from four points in this way are known as Bezier curves, after a mathematician called Pierre Bezier.

You have complete control over Bezier curves. You can draw lines with as many curves as you like and, once you have drawn a curved line, you can adjust it in several ways. For example, you can make the curve deeper, shallower or lean to one side, by dragging the control points to new positions.

These pictures show how a curve is controlled by four points.

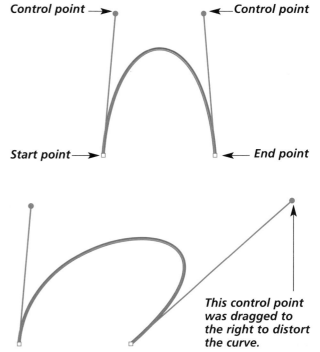

Control point →

← Control point

Start point →

← End point

This control point was dragged to the right to distort the curve.

Drawing skills

This section shows you some of the more exciting things that can be done with drawing programs.

Layers

With some drawing programs, you can divide a picture up into different "layers". This is useful when you create very detailed pictures with lots of overlapping shapes.

The first layer you create is the bottom layer. The other layers are laid over the top to build up a picture. It may help to think of each layer

of the picture as a piece of transparent paper with a drawing on it.

You can instruct a drawing program to show and hide layers as you please. To work on a shape which is on one of the bottom layers, you would first need to instruct the program to hide the top layers.

Because drawing programs consider each shape or line you create to be a separate object, you can easily move a shape or line from one layer to another.

A picture made from four layers

These are the four separate layers that make up the picture.

The leaves are on the fourth layer.

The third layer contains the tiger.

The bush is on the second layer.

Here, all the layers are visible.

The first layer contains only the sky.

Ready-made patterns

Drawing programs often include a library of ready-made patterns. You can use these to fill in the shapes you draw. You can also create your own patterns to add to the library. One useful kind of pattern is called a gradient. It contains two or more colors that gradually merge.

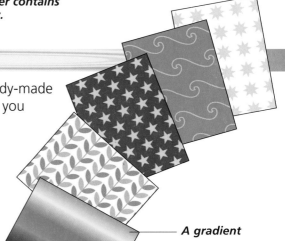

A selection of the patterns that come with Adobe Illustrator 7.0

A gradient

Metamorphosis

Some drawing programs can transform one object into another. In Adobe Illustrator, for example, this process is called blending. In CorelDRAW it is called transforming.

To turn one object, such as a black tadpole shape, into another, such as a green frog shape, a drawing program draws a number of shapes in between the tadpole and the frog. These shapes show the gradual transformation of the tadpole into the frog.

You can specify how many shapes you want to appear in between the first and the last. The drawing program will calculate the shape, color and position of each one and then draw it on screen.

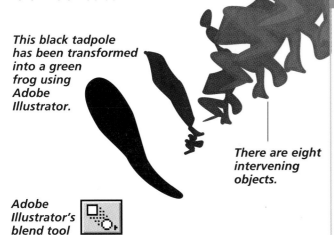

This black tadpole has been transformed into a green frog using Adobe Illustrator.

There are eight intervening objects.

Adobe Illustrator's blend tool

Saving vector graphics

Unless you specify otherwise, drawing programs will automatically save pictures in their own file formats. For example, Adobe Illustrator saves graphics as **.ai** files and CorelDRAW saves them as **.cdr** files.

A file format that a program uses automatically is known as a native file format.

Graphics tablets

It is not easy to draw accurately with a mouse. Many computer artists prefer to use a kind of drawing board called a graphics tablet, and an electronic pen called a stylus. The artist draws with the stylus on the tablet. Most tablets are pressure-sensitive. This means they respond to increases in pressure on the stylus by creating thicker or darker lines. So drawing with a graphics tablet and stylus is similar to drawing with pencil and paper.

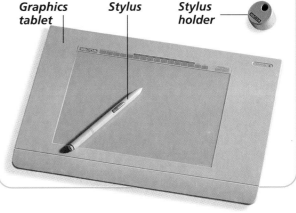

Graphics tablet   *Stylus*   *Stylus holder*

Putting pictures into a computer

You can use graphics software to change or "edit" pictures, such as photographs or drawings, that weren't created on a computer.

Before you can do this though, you need to convert the picture into a form that a computer can handle, and for this, you need to use a machine called a scanner.

About scanners

A scanner collects information about a picture and stores the information as computer data. This process is called scanning, and a picture to be scanned is known as an original.

There are three main types of scanners: drum scanners, flatbed scanners and sheet-fed scanners. Drum scanners are big machines which can scan several originals at once. They are used by businesses, such as newspaper printers, that need to scan a lot of pictures. Flatbed scanners and sheet-fed scanners are both small enough to use at home, at school or in an office.

Digital images

Computers store and process information as numbers, or digits. The word "digital" is used to describe information that is represented by numbers. The process of turning a piece of information into numbers is called digitizing. Any picture that has been created on a computer, or that has been scanned in, is called a digital image.

Below is a sheet-fed scanner.

The original is scanned as it passes through the scanner.

You can only scan pictures on single sheets of paper with a sheet-fed scanner.

The lid must be closed while scanning takes place.

Using a flatbed scanner

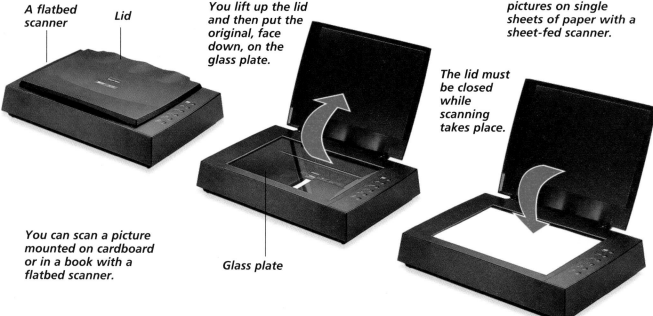

A flatbed scanner

Lid

You lift up the lid and then put the original, face down, on the glass plate.

You can scan a picture mounted on cardboard or in a book with a flatbed scanner.

Glass plate

What does a scanner do?

A scanner divides a picture into a grid of pixels. A light inside the scanner shines on the picture, and a small electronic device called a charge-coupled device (CCD) records how much light each pixel reflects and reports this information to a computer. Once the computer has all the information, it creates a digital copy of the picture and displays it on screen.

Below you can see how a flatbed scanner collects information about a picture.

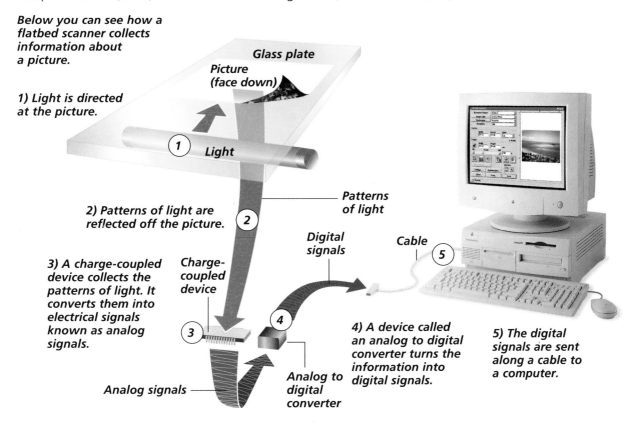

Glass plate

Picture (face down)

1) Light is directed at the picture.

1

Light

2) Patterns of light are reflected off the picture.

2

Patterns of light

Digital signals

Cable

5

3) A charge-coupled device collects the patterns of light. It converts them into electrical signals known as analog signals.

Charge-coupled device

3

4

4) A device called an analog to digital converter turns the information into digital signals.

5) The digital signals are sent along a cable to a computer.

Analog signals

Analog to digital converter

Digital cameras

Another way of putting pictures into your computer is by using a digital camera. This is a camera that captures scenes directly as digital images. It uses a charge-coupled device to detect patterns of light and then stores them in its memory.

A digital camera comes with a cable so it can be attached to your computer. This allows you to transfer the photographs stored in the camera to your computer's hard disk so that you can edit them or print them out.

A digital camera

A scanner only works when it is connected to a computer and operated by software on that computer. You can use two types of software: a program that is used only for scanning, or imaging software (see page 24).

Preparing to scan

The first stage in scanning a picture is to produce a rough scan or "preview" of your picture. You may have to instruct a scanner to do this, or it may do it automatically. The preview appears in a dialog box similar to the one on the right. You use this dialog box to specify exactly how you would like your picture to be scanned a second time. For example, you can choose whether the scanner scans the whole picture, or only a part of it.

A dialog box from some scanning software

Use this list box to specify whether the picture is black and white or color.

Type in the dimensions of the picture here.

Preview

Scanning resolution

When you are preparing to scan, one of the things you will need to specify is the number of pixels into which the scanner will divide the picture. This is known as the scanning resolution. It is measured in pixels per inch (ppi), although many people mistakenly say dots per inch (dpi). (One inch is 2.5 cm.)

Most scanners can scan at different resolutions, ranging from 72 or 75 ppi up to 300 ppi. Resolution is described as low or high. 72 ppi is a low resolution and 300 ppi is a high resolution.

High resolution scans contain more pixels than low resolution scans, so they produce bigger files. They don't look any better than low resolution scans when they are displayed on a computer screen. So if you are only going to look at a picture on screen, it is a good idea to scan it at a low resolution to save disk space. However, high resolution scans look better than low resolution scans when they are printed out. If you are going to print out your pictures, you should scan them at 150 ppi or higher.

These printouts of digital images show the effects of scanning at different resolutions.

This is a high resolution scan. You can't see the individual pixels.

This is a low resolution scan. The pixels are easy to see.

Scanning

Once you have set up a scan, click on the button or menu item in the scanning software that instructs the scanner to start scanning. It may take a few minutes for the scanner to scan the whole picture and transmit the data to the computer. When it has finished, the computer will display a copy of the picture in a new window, like the one shown below.

Saving a scanned image

Once you have scanned an original, you should save the digital image you have created before you start making changes to it. That way if you don't like the changes you make, you will be able to start anew without having to scan the picture again.

To save a digital image, select *Save* from the *File* menu. Use the Save As dialog box that appears to choose a name, file format and location for the file.

Scanning programs allow you to save images in various raster file formats. It is a good idea to save scanned images in the Tagged Image File Format (TIFF) (see page 35).

Getting access to a scanner

If you decide to buy a scanner, make sure you choose one that you can connect to your computer. A scanner connects to a socket or "port" at the back of a computer's system unit. (This is the box that contains the on/off button.) There are different types of ports. Check your computer's manual to see what type of scanner you need.

Instead of buying a scanner, you can have your pictures digitized by a business that provides scanning, printing and copying services. This is known as a service bureau. You pay to have your pictures scanned and saved onto floppy disk or CD.

Scanners come with cables like these for connecting them to your computer.

You can also have photographs digitized when you have a roll of film developed by a photograph processing business. Your photographs will be returned to you on a kind of CD called a PhotoCD.

A PhotoCD comes with an "index print". This shows a tiny printed version of each picture stored on the CD.

The index print fits inside a CD case.

Each picture is accompanied by a number to help you find it on the CD.

A PhotoCD looks like any other CD.

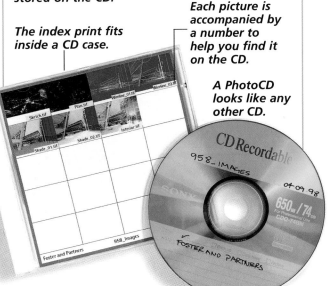

Once a picture, such as a photograph, has been put into your computer, you can alter it using a type of graphics software known either as image manipulation software, image-editing software or imaging software.

Imaging programs

Many professional computer artists and graphic designers use an imaging program called Adobe® Photoshop® . A less expensive program is Jasc's Paint Shop Pro. Its window is shown below.

A Paint Shop Pro window

Tool bar   **Tool palette**

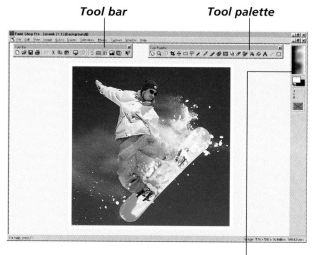

Color palette

Improving images

You can use imaging software to make a digital image look better. For example, it lets you clean up blemishes on a picture, such as specks of dirt that have been picked up by the scanner.

Once you have cleaned up your image, save the file before you make any further changes to it. If you don't like the changes you make, you will be able to start over without having to clean up the picture again.

Cropping

In computer graphics, trimming a picture to the size and shape you require is called cropping.

To crop a picture to a rectangular shape in most imaging programs, including Paint Shop Pro, you use a tool called the Crop tool. To crop a picture to an irregular shape in Paint Shop Pro, you first use a selection tool to select the area you want to save. Then choose the *Crop to Selection* command from the *Image* menu. This instructs the program to delete the rest of the picture. With other programs, you may need to use a different method to crop a picture to an irregular shape.

A photograph before it has been cropped

The picture on the left was created by selecting a rectangular shape, then cropping the photograph.

The picture on the right was created by selecting an irregular shape, then cropping the photograph.

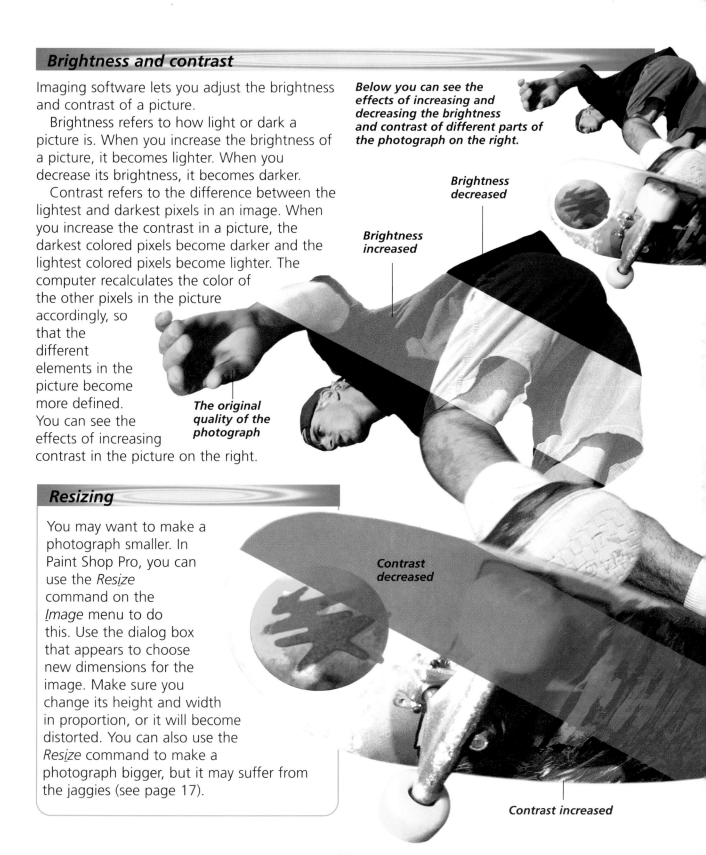

Brightness and contrast

Imaging software lets you adjust the brightness and contrast of a picture.

Brightness refers to how light or dark a picture is. When you increase the brightness of a picture, it becomes lighter. When you decrease its brightness, it becomes darker.

Contrast refers to the difference between the lightest and darkest pixels in an image. When you increase the contrast in a picture, the darkest colored pixels become darker and the lightest colored pixels become lighter. The computer recalculates the color of the other pixels in the picture accordingly, so that the different elements in the picture become more defined. You can see the effects of increasing contrast in the picture on the right.

Below you can see the effects of increasing and decreasing the brightness and contrast of different parts of the photograph on the right.

Brightness decreased

Brightness increased

The original quality of the photograph

Resizing

You may want to make a photograph smaller. In Paint Shop Pro, you can use the *Resize* command on the *Image* menu to do this. Use the dialog box that appears to choose new dimensions for the image. Make sure you change its height and width in proportion, or it will become distorted. You can also use the *Resize* command to make a photograph bigger, but it may suffer from the jaggies (see page 17).

Contrast decreased

Contrast increased

Imaging software gives you the power to perform clever tricks with photographs. You can select any shape with a single click of your mouse, make people and objects disappear, or conjure up impossible scenes.

Magic Wand

Many imaging programs include a selection tool called a Magic Wand. This selects any shape formed by a group of pixels that are the same color. You don't have to draw around the shape. For example, if you click on a red pixel in one of the diamonds on a picture of a playing card, the Magic Wand will select all the red pixels that make up that diamond. It will not select any other red pixels in the picture.

In this picture, the Magic Wand has been used to select a diamond shape.

The Magic Wand was clicked here.

Paint Shop Pro's Magic Wand tool

Magic Wand options

A Magic Wand tool includes an option called Tolerance or Similarity. You use this to specify how close a color match the Magic Wand should look for when it is selecting pixels.

When a Magic Wand's Tolerance setting is 0, it will look for a perfect color match. For example, if you click on a yellow pixel, it will select only those pixels which are exactly the same shade of yellow. By increasing the Tolerance number, you can instruct the Magic Wand to select pixels which are a similar shade of yellow as well.

These pictures show the results of clicking on a yellow pixel with a Magic Wand at different Tolerance settings.

Original picture

The Magic Wand was clicked here.

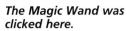

If the Tolerance is 0, the Magic Wand selects only a few pixels.

When the Tolerance is 20, the Magic Wand selects the yellow area shown above.

When the Tolerance is 60, the Magic Wand selects all the yellow pixels in the picture.

Composite images

A composite image is a picture that is made from cutting out parts of other pictures and pasting them together.

You can produce all kinds of weird and wonderful composite images.

Compositing can be used to make it look as if two people or animals have had their photograph taken together, even if they have never met.

This picture was made from two completely separate photographs.

Retouching photographs

Photo-retouching means removing or "editing out" part of a picture and replacing it with something else. One way of doing this is by copying some pixels from one part of a picture and using them to replace an unwanted part.

For example, you could copy the blue areas of a sky scene and use them to cover up any clouds to create a perfect blue sky. Copying pixels is known as cloning. Most imaging programs have a tool for cloning.

Cloning was one of several imaging techniques used to produce this picture of a man floating in mid-air.

A photograph before retouching

The retouched photograph

These supports hold the man in position.

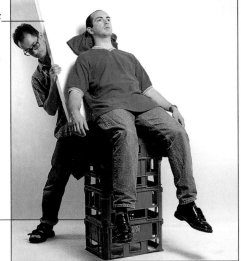

Pixels have been copied from this part of the photograph and used to cover up the supports.

Filters

Imaging programs include tools called filters, which enable you to transform a picture's appearance completely.

Filters

In photography, a filter is a device which a photographer places over the lens of a camera to change the way light enters the camera. This alters the way the camera captures a scene. Photographers can filter light in different ways, to add a variety of interesting effects to their photographs.

In computer graphics, a filter is a tool that transforms an existing picture. Using a filter on a picture is known as applying a filter. When you apply a filter to a picture, the graphics program uses a mathematical formula to change the data that describes the picture.

Some filters copy effects that can be achieved in photography. Others create special effects that can't be achieved with a camera.

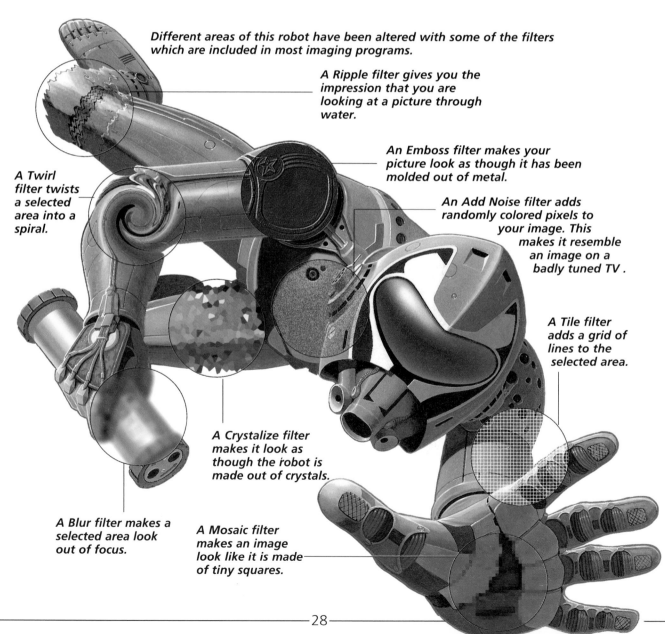

Different areas of this robot have been altered with some of the filters which are included in most imaging programs.

A Ripple filter gives you the impression that you are looking at a picture through water.

An Emboss filter makes your picture look as though it has been molded out of metal.

A Twirl filter twists a selected area into a spiral.

An Add Noise filter adds randomly colored pixels to your image. This makes it resemble an image on a badly tuned TV .

A Tile filter adds a grid of lines to the selected area.

A Crystalize filter makes it look as though the robot is made out of crystals.

A Blur filter makes a selected area look out of focus.

A Mosaic filter makes an image look like it is made of tiny squares.

Applying filters

You can apply most filters to the whole image, or just a part of it. To apply a filter, select the area of the image that you want it to affect, then click on the filter command, for example *Blur*.

In most imaging programs, you will find the filter commands on the *Filter* menu. In Paint Shop Pro, you will find three filter submenus under the *Image* menu.

Giving details

You may have to complete a dialog box to specify exactly how you would like a particular filter to be applied. For example, with the Mosaic filter shown on the opposite page, you need to type in numbers to specify how wide and how high you would like the pieces of the mosaic to be. If you aren't sure how you want a filter to be applied, experiment with different numbers until you achieve an effect you like.

Paint Shop Pro's Mosaic dialog box

A preview of the effect the filter will produce.

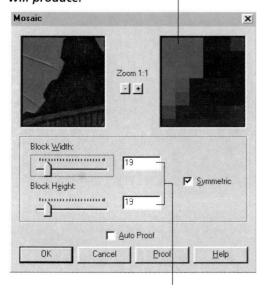

Type in new numbers here to alter the effect.

Extra filters

You don't just have to stick to the filters provided with your imaging program. You can obtain extra filters in the form of "plug-ins". A plug-in is a piece of software that you can add to another program, and which can only work with other programs. Popular plug-in filters which work with imaging programs include Kai's Power Tools and Adobe® Gallery Effects® .

There are also small programs that include only a few specific filters. These programs work by themselves so you don't have to have an imaging program to experiment with the filters they contain.

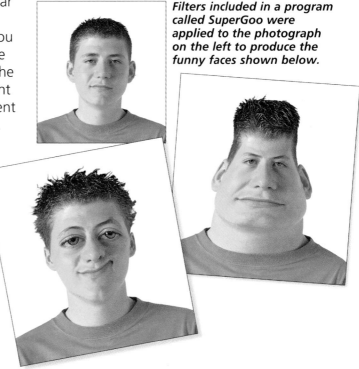

Filters included in a program called SuperGoo were applied to the photograph on the left to produce the funny faces shown below.

⚠ Try not to get carried away when adding plug-ins to your imaging program. Plug-ins use up a lot of "Random Access Memory" (RAM). This is the part of your computer's memory that enables it to use programs. When you add plug-ins to your imaging program, the program will work more slowly than usual.

Printing your pictures

These pages contain essential information about printing out computer graphics.

Print resolution

Printed images are made up of thousands of dots - the smaller the dots, the sharper and clearer the image. The sharpness of a printed image is called print resolution, and it is measured in dots per inch (dpi).

Types of printers

The most popular printers for home and office use are inkjet printers (also called bubblejet printers) and laser printers. Color printers and black and white printers of both types are available.

   Laser printers print at a resolution of between 300 and 600 dpi. This means they can produce sharper images than inkjet printers, which can only print at a resolution of 300 dpi. Laser printers also print faster than inkjet printers. However, they are more expensive.

Printing colors

To produce full color pictures, a color printer combines four different colored inks - cyan (a kind of turquoise), magenta (bright pink), yellow and black. Graphic designers use a color model (see page 13) called the CMYK color model to describe colors according to the amounts of cyan, magenta, yellow and black they contain.

Yellow

Cyan

Magenta

Black

Color chaos

Colors printed out on paper often do not look the same as they appear on screen. One of the reasons for this is that printers use a different color model from monitors. In addition, the colors that a monitor displays are affected by the lighting in the room and the monitor's age. Colors look duller on older monitors than they do on brand new ones.

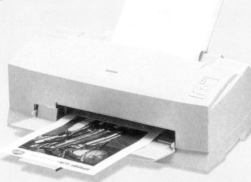

A color inkjet printer

A piece of paper that a printer has printed on is called a printout.

An inkjet printer makes pictures by spraying tiny droplets of liquid ink onto paper. Allow the paper to dry for a few seconds before you remove it.

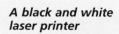

A black and white laser printer

A laser printer uses powdered ink called toner which sticks to the paper.

Printing services

If you don't have a printer, or you want better results than your printer can produce, you can take a file to a printing service (see page 23) to have it printed out.

Preparing to print

Start by displaying the picture you want to print in the graphics program in which you created or altered it. Next, select _Print..._ from the _File_ menu. A Print dialog box will appear.

Use the Print dialog box to specify how you want the printer to print the picture. For example, you will need to state how many copies you want. You may need to click on a button called _Properties_ or _Options_ to see all the available options. When you have completed the dialog box, click _OK_.

You can have the paper one of two ways. These are known as orientations.

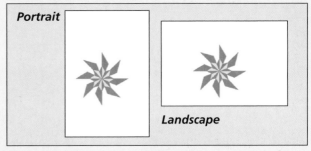

Portrait

Landscape

Click to select the orientation of the paper.

A print dialog box

Click here to see more options.

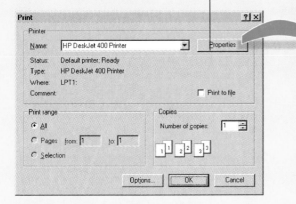

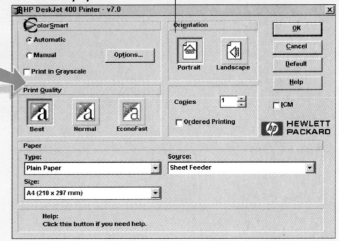

Printing

Your computer uses a type of programming language called a Page Description Language (PDL) to tell a printer exactly how to draw a picture on paper. Most laser printers use a PDL called Adobe PostScript. While your computer is sending a description of a picture to the printer, you will see a progress window on your screen.

A printer will only start printing once it has received and processed all the information about the picture. This may take some time. Don't turn off your computer or your printer while you are waiting, as this could damage the software that controls your printer.

A progress window

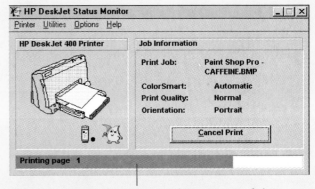

This growing bar represents the amount of data that has already been sent to the printer.

Importing and exporting graphics

You can alter or include a graphic created in one program in another program. For example, you can change a picture drawn in Paint (see page 4) by using an imaging program (see page 24).

By using more than one program, you can produce different kinds of pictures and documents. Opening a computer file in a program other than the one that was used to create it is known as importing.

Here are some of the types of documents you can produce by working on a picture in more than one program:

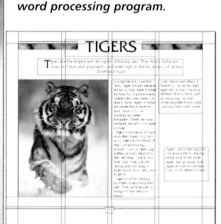

To produce this invitation, the photograph was imported into a word processing program.

This is the photograph that has been used in all of the documents shown on the right.

This poster was created by importing a logo and words designed in a drawing program into an imaging program.

To design this page of a book, the photograph was imported into special software for designing page layouts called desktop publishing (DTP) software.

File formats

Pictures can be saved in different file formats (this is the way a graphics program arranges the data on disk). The main graphics formats are listed on page 33. Most graphics programs can work with, or "support", more than one file format. For example, Microsoft Paint can support Microsoft bitmaps, GIF and JPEG formats. You will find information about which file formats a program supports in the manual that comes with it, or in its Help system.

Exporting

Before you can import a picture into a program, you may need to save it in a different format first. Saving a file in a different format so that another program can handle it is known as exporting. For example, to open a picture which is saved as a TIFF in Paint, you first need to export the picture into a file format that Paint supports, such as Microsoft bitmap, GIF or JPEG. You can find out how to do this on page 33.

Common graphics formats

When choosing a file format for a picture, it is helpful to know about different graphics file formats. The format you choose will depend on what you want to do with your picture or which program you want to import it into.

Here are some common graphics file formats. Many graphics programs, and some other types of programs, such as desktop publishing programs, support these file formats.

gif Graphics Interchange Format (GIF). This format is popular for pictures that are transferred across the Internet (see page 34). It can only contain up to 256 colors, so it is usually used for simple cartoons, icons and line drawings.

pcd Kodak PhotoCD format. When you have a roll of film containing photographs taken by a camera developed onto a PhotoCD (see page 23), the photographs will be stored in this format.

tiff Tagged Image File Format (TIFF). This format is supported by a wide range of programs and computer systems. It is used for transferring pictures between different kinds of programs. For example, it is popular for images that are to be imported into desktop publishing programs.

eps Encapsulated PostScript (EPS). This format can contain information about both bitmap graphics and vector graphics. The information is stored in Adobe PostScript (see page 31). EPS format is often used for importing files into desktop publishing programs.

jpeg Joint Photographics Experts Group (JPEG) format. This format is commonly used for pictures that are transferred across the Internet, in particular those containing many different colors such a photographs, illustrations and paintings. Find out more on page 35.

How to export a file

To export a file, open the file in the program in which it was created. If the graphics program you are using has an *Export* command on the *File* menu, select this command. A menu of file formats that you can choose from will appear.

Alternatively, if the program you are using does not have an *Export* command, select *Save As* from the *File* menu. The file formats you can choose from appear in a drop down list at the bottom of the Save As dialog box. Choose a file format that the other program supports and click *OK*.

Exporting a file creates a copy of the file in a different format. The original file remains unchanged.

Switching systems

A particular computer system, such as a PC controlled by the Microsoft Windows operating system, or a Mac controlled by the Mac operating system, is known as a platform.

The file formats described above are not only supported by many different programs, but also by different platforms. A file format or program that can be supported by different platforms is described as platform independent.

This Apple iMac™ computer is controlled by the Mac operating system.

Graphics on screen

Some graphics are created specifically to be seen on a computer screen. They are prepared in a different way from graphics that are used in books and other printed material.

Screen pictures

You will find graphics that have been designed for the screen in many places, including computer games, multimedia CD-ROMs, information kiosks (like the one shown below right) and on the World Wide Web or "Web". The Web is a huge collection of information available on a worldwide network of computers known as the Internet.

A screen from a multimedia CD-ROM

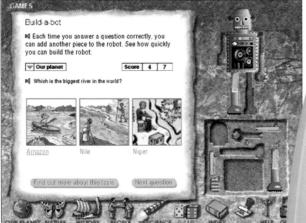

Multimedia CD-ROMs contain information in many different forms such as words, pictures, moving images and sounds.

A page of information from the World Wide Web. The information on the Web is stored on Internet computers all over the world.

Below is a kiosk which is a computer system for use by people visiting museums, shopping centers and libraries.

Visitors touch the screen to request information.

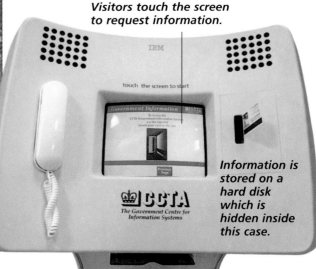

Information is stored on a hard disk which is hidden inside this case.

Saving time

People using the systems shown above expect information, such as computer graphics, to appear on screen quickly. To achieve this, the graphics files have to be as small as possible. This is because a computer has to process the data in a file in order to display the graphic. The smaller the file, the less time this takes.

It is particularly important to keep graphics files that are used on the World Wide Web small. When someone uses the Web, their computer has to copy a file from the Internet computer on which it is stored before it can process the data in the file. Copying files across the Internet can be a slow process.

Saving space

Sometimes, people need to store computer files on a storage device which has limited space. For example, all the information for a multimedia CD-ROM – text, sound, pictures, animation and video – must fit onto a single CD-ROM.

The smaller a file is, the less storage space it takes up. Designers make graphics files for games and multimedia CD-ROMs small to fit them into the storage space available.

Low resolution scans

One way of reducing the size of a graphics file is to scan photographs and pictures at a low resolution, such as 72ppi (see page 22). This won't affect the way the image looks on screen, because monitors can only display images at a low resolution. Another way is to limit the number of colors in the picture (see page 15).

Compression

You can also reduce the size of a file by instructing your computer to store the information in a way that takes up less space on a disk. This process is known as compression. There are two ways of compressing a graphics file. One way is to use a piece of software called a compression program. The other way is to choose a file format that compresses a file as it saves it, such as JPEG format (see page 33).

Compression programs

A compression program can compress any type of file. Three popular compression programs are PKZIP, WinZip and StuffIt. When you use a compression program to compress a file, it doesn't throw away any of the data. This means you can restore a file compressed with a compression program to its original size.

JPEG compression

JPEG format compresses files by removing some of the information they contain. This is known as lossy compression. It starts by throwing away pixels that are invisible to the human eye. The more a JPEG file is compressed, the easier it is to see the differences between the original file and the compressed version.

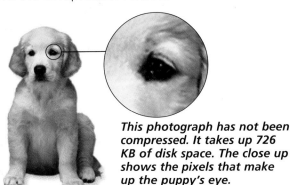

This photograph has not been compressed. It takes up 726 KB of disk space. The close up shows the pixels that make up the puppy's eye.

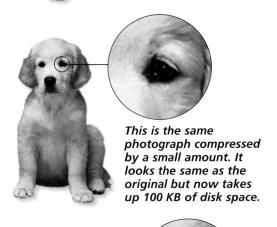

This is the same photograph compressed by a small amount. It looks the same as the original but now takes up 100 KB of disk space.

Here the photograph has been compressed as much as possible. The file is only 43 KB but you can tell that some of the pixels have been removed.

Computer animation

Computers can bring pictures to life by making them appear to move. This process is known as computer animation.

Animated computer graphics are used to present information in an interesting way or for pure entertainment.

These pictures show some of the different uses of animated computer graphics.

This computer animation decorates the Usborne Publishing Web page.

A computer-animated TV advertisement

A cartoon called Mungie which was animated using computers

Animated pictures called screen savers appear on a computer screen when the computer isn't used for a while.

A screen shot from a CD-ROM called Puzzle Castle which contains animated characters.

A mouse pointer can appear as an animated picture.

An animated character from a computer game called Jazz JackRabbit

Deceiving our eyes

Animation works by fooling the human eye. An animation is made from a sequence of pictures called frames. Each frame is slightly different from the previous one.

When the frames are shown one after the other very quickly, your eyes see a single, moving picture.

For the objects and characters to appear to move smoothly, a sequence of 24 different frames must be shown every second. The number of frames shown in one second of an animation is called the frame rate. It is measured in frames per second (fps).

A bouncing ball animation

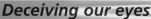

A frame

Planning a story

The first stage in creating an animation is to plan out what will happen. An animator produces a series of sketches on paper of the main events in an animation. These sketches are called a storyboard.

Sketches from a storyboard for a cartoon called **Rolie Polie Olie**

A picture from the finished cartoon

Key frames

The next step is to produce computer graphics for the "key frames" of the animation. These are the frames that show the beginning or the end of a particular movement. For a falling tree, for example, one key frame would show the tree standing upright and the other would show it lying on the ground.

Some animators create key frames by drawing directly on a computer. Others start by drawing outlines for the key frames on paper. Then they scan in these outlines (see page 20) and color them in on a computer with imaging software.

In between frames

Next, the animator imports the completed key frames into animation software, which can create the rest of the frames for the animation by itself.

 — *Key frame*

The animator tells the software exactly when each key frame should appear in the animation. To do this, the animator sets a time for each key frame on a clock. The clock is set at 0 seconds for the first frame.

The software then calculates how many frames it must create to appear in between the key frames, and what they will look like. It then creates all the frames. This process is known as inbetweening or tweening.

In between frames

Before computers were used in animation, every single frame had to be drawn and colored in by hand. Now computers can save animators hours of work by generating inbetween frames for them.

 — *Key frame*

Inbetween frames produced by animation software called the Animo® system

You can create your own animated pictures with a program called a GIF animation editor. This can bring together a series of pictures to form an animation.

GIF Animator

The GIF animation editor used in this example is called GIF Animator. You can obtain a free trial version of GIF Animator which will work for 15 days. (Find out how on page 70.) If you want to continue using the program after the trial period, you will have to buy a proper copy.

GIF Animator is less expensive than animation programs used by professional animators. However, you will need to create all the frames for your animation by yourself. To do this, you can use any painting or drawing program.

Creating the frames

Start by creating a new folder called *animation* on your computer's hard disk. This is where you will save each frame as you draw it.

Draw the first frame and save it with a name that indicates its postion in the sequence, such as **frame1**. Choose one of the following file formats – GIF, JPEG, TIFF or Microsoft Bitmap. To create the second frame, alter **frame1** slightly. Use the *Save As...* command to save it with a different name. Continue this process until you have created all the frames.

The first two frames of an animation of a jet flying in a loop

jet2.jpg

jet1.jpg

Starting up

When you have finished preparing the frames, open your GIF Animator program. (If you have a trial version, you will see a window which reminds you how many more days you have to try the program. Click *Try More!* to continue.)

A window called Startup Wizard will appear. To start a new animation, click on the icon next to *Blank Animation*. The main GIF Animator window will appear on your screen. The bottom part of the window is divided into two areas, known as the Layer Pane and the workspace.

Gif Animator's window   Tool bar

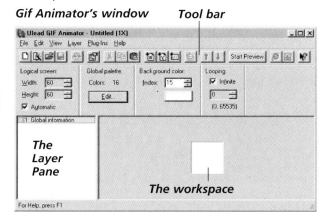

The Layer Pane

The workspace

Bringing in the frames

To bring the frames for your animation into GIF Animator, click on the Add Image button on the tool bar. The Add Images dialog box will open. Locate the frames in your *animation* folder, select them and click *Open*.

The Add Images dialog box

Add Image button

This box shows a preview of the currently selected frame.

Organizing the frames

All the frames that you selected will be listed in the Layer Pane. If necessary, use your mouse to drag the names of the frames into the correct order for your animation.

A section of the main window showing the Layer Pane

Make sure the first frame appears at the top of the list and the last frame at the bottom.

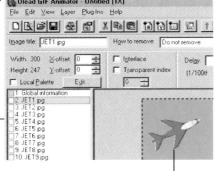

The selected frame is shown in the workspace.

You can now watch a preview of your animation in the workspace. To do this, click the *Start Preview* button on the tool bar. To end the preview, click the *Stop Preview* button.

Your animation will play over and over again until you click the Stop Preview button.

Frame rate

GIF Animator measures the length of time each frame of an animation appears on screen in hundredths of a second. Unless instructed otherwise, it will display each frame for 10 hundredths of a second. This is the same as a frame rate of 10 fps. When an animation's frame rate is 25 fps, each frame is displayed for 4 hundredths of a second.

Adjusting the frame rate

In GIF Animator, a control called *Delay* sets the length of time for which a frame is displayed during an animation.

To alter this, select the name of the particular frame from the list in the Layer Pane. A *Delay* control for that frame will appear. The number in the little box states how many hundredths of seconds the frame will appear for. To display a frame for longer, increase the number. To move on to the next frame more quickly, decrease the number.

GIF Animator's Delay control

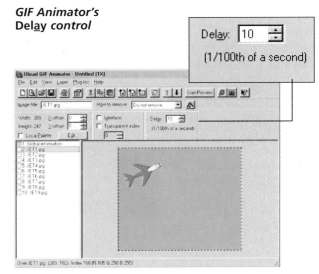

Saving your animation

To save your animation, select *Save* from the *File* menu and complete the Save As dialog box. When you have finished, click *OK*. GIF Animator will save your animation as a GIF file.

When you click *OK*, GIF Animator will also start up a help system called the *Optimization Wizard*. This can reduce the size of the GIF file as it saves it. If you intend to put your animation on the World Wide Web (see page 34), it's a good idea to use the Optimization Wizard. If not, click *Cancel* to close the Optimization Wizard.

Morphing is a way of transforming one shape into another smoothly. It is often used in music videos and movies to change someone's appearance or turn one character into another. For example, the video featured on the right showed a series of faces morphing into one another. It can also be used to turn a person into an object, or transform one object into another. A moving image that shows a transformation like this is known as a morph.

Morphing was used in the video for a song called **Black or White** *by* **Michael Jackson.**

A sequence from **Willow (1988),** *the first feature film to use morphing*

A turtle is turning into a tiger. The feet change first.

This picture shows a half turtle, half tiger creature.

Here it has been completely transformed into a tiger.

This morph was produced with a program called MorphMan.

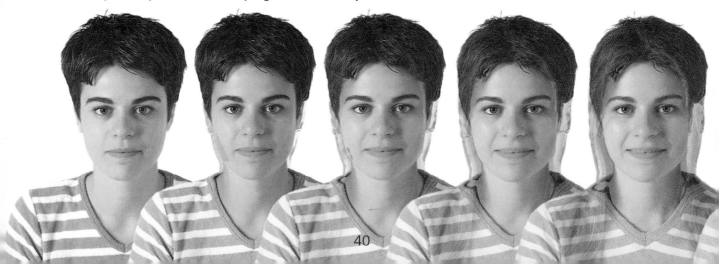

Morphing software

Morphs are made using morphing software. In a morph, the picture that is transformed is called the start or source picture. The picture into which the source picture is transformed is called the end or target picture.

These are the source and target pictures for the morph shown across the bottom of these pages.

Source

Target

Morphing software produces a series of pictures that are part way between the source and target pictures. When all the pictures are displayed one after another, very quickly, the source appears to turn into the target.

Try it out

You can try out morphing yourself with a program called MorphMan. A free demonstration copy of this progam is available. Find out how to get it on page 70.

Selecting points and lines

In a morphing program, you start by choosing and marking important areas on the source picture by positioning points and lines. For example, on a picture of a face, you might position a point on each of the eyes and a line around the curve of the chin.

Then, for each point or line on the source picture, you must position a matching point or line on the target picture. For each matching pair of points or lines, the morphing program will transform the point or line in the source picture into the point or line in the target picture. The more points and lines you mark, the smoother your morph will be.

Two pictures with matching points and lines

Matching points

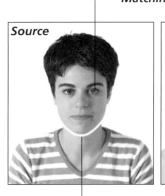
Source

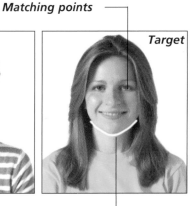
Target

Matching lines

Working with video

Making changes to videos is called video editing. A computer can be used to edit videos that have been recorded with a video camera. It can remove unwanted sections of video, or join one section to another smoothly.

Video editing requires a computer with a hard disk that is larger than the average home or school computer's hard disk, some video hardware, and some video editing software.

Putting video into a computer

Some video cameras record videos onto magnetic tape which is stored in removable cassettes. To copy a video from a cassette, a computer must contain a device called a video capture card, and be connected to a video camera or video cassette player. As the video cassette player or video camera plays the video, the video capture card turns the information on the tape into computer data.

A video capture card

Video is made from a series of still images called frames. A video capture card creates a digital image for each frame of video.

Video appears on the computer screen as a series of still images called frames.

A frame ——————

Digital video cameras

Some video cameras, known as digital video cameras, don't use cassettes. Instead, they record video onto a hard disk, which is similar to the hard disk inside a computer.

A computer still needs a video capture card to transfer a video from the hard disk inside a digital video camera to its own hard disk.

A digital video camera

Editing a video

Once a video is stored on a computer, video editing software can be used to make changes to it. Video editors can change the order of the frames in a video and delete any frames they don't need. They can also add sounds and special effects. One popular video editing program is called Adobe®Premiere®.

Below is a screen shot from Adobe Premiere.

These buttons play back a video.

Frames can be dragged to a new position with a mouse.

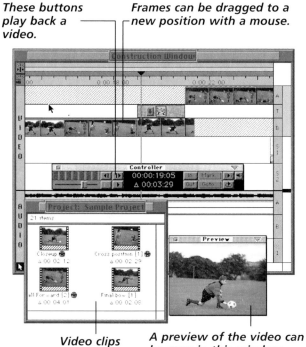

Video clips

A preview of the video can be seen in this window.

Transitions

In video editing, a link between the end of one series of frames and the beginning of another is known as a transition. Most video editing programs provide a variety of interesting ways of carrying out transitions. These are known as transition effects.

One type of transition effect is a wipe, in which one image gradually covers up another one, producing a pattern as it does so. Other transition effects include fades and page turns.

Two common transition effects

A wipe ***A page turn***

Special effects

Digital video can be manipulated in the same way as digital photographs. For example, filters (see page 28) can be applied and unwanted objects can be painted out.

Most video editing programs include a few filters and other special effects. There are also plug-ins (see page 29) to add to the choice of filters and special effects.

These pictures show the effect of a Wind filter.

This is the frame before the filter was applied.

This is the frame after the filter has been applied.

Finishing

There are two ways of saving a finished video. It can either be saved as a computer file or transferred onto video tape.

To watch a video stored as a computer file, you need a program called a multimedia player. To copy video onto video tape, a computer needs a type of video capture card called a two-way or in/out card. Once a video is on tape, it can be played on a video cassette player.

Hardware requirements

To work with video in the ways described on these pages, your computer needs at least 4 gigabytes of hard disk space. (A gigabyte is just over 1000 megabytes.)

Before you buy a video editing program, make sure that your computer matches the minimum requirements listed on the box.

Special effects

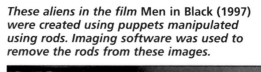

M any special effects in movies and television are created using computers. Special effects that are produced in this way are known as digital effects.

Digital effects are usually created after a piece of action has been filmed. The moving images are put into a computer and imaging software (see page 24) is used to alter individual frames.

Here are some of the ways in which computers are used in special effects.

These aliens in the film Men in Black (1997) *were created using puppets manipulated using rods. Imaging software was used to remove the rods from these images.*

Creating crowds

Everyone taking part in a crowd scene has to wear a costume and be paid. This makes large crowd scenes difficult and expensive to organize. Instead, film makers can use a process known as crowd multiplication to turn a group of a hundred people into a crowd of thousands.

Crowd multiplication involves a special effects technique called compositing. This is the process of combining parts of a number of separate film shots into one shot. To multiply a crowd, film makers film several versions of a scene. For each version, the crowd moves to a different position. Then all the versions are put into a computer. Digital effects experts produce a composite image by cutting out the crowd from the different versions and pasting them together.

For the movie Braveheart (1995) *a group of actors was filmed on the left of the battlefield, and then the same group was filmed on the right of the battlefield. The two shots were then combined to produce the image shown below.*

Changing backgrounds

Compositing is also used to put actors or objects filmed against a plain background in front of a different background. This may be another piece of film, a painting, or a computer-generated scene.

For *Lost in Space (1998)*, a model of a spacecraft was filmed against a plain green background. This image was then combined with an outer space background.

To do this, the shot of the spacecraft was put into a computer. A digital effects expert cut out the spacecraft's shape on each frame by covering up the green background with a device called a mask. This mask was also used to cut a spacecraft-shaped hole in the outer space background. Finally, the two part-images were fitted together to produce a composite image (see page 27).

Below are pictures from the making of the film **Lost in Space.**

Detailed designs for this spacecraft were produced on a computer before a model of it was built.

This is a shot of the spacecraft against a green background.

A green support was used to hold the model in place.

In this scene, shots of the model have been composited with a space background.

3-D graphics

Three dimensional (3-D) computer graphics are pictures in which objects and scenes appear to have depth as well as height and width. 3-D graphics have many uses, ranging from computer games to scientific research. They are also used in Virtual Reality (see pages 60 to 63).

Business graphics

Many businesses use computer graphics to communicate information, such as statistics, visually. There are computer programs which can convert numbers into graphs or charts. Some of these programs produce 3-D graphics. Computer graphics that show information in a way that is interesting to look at are known as presentation graphics.

This 3-D pie chart was created using a presentation graphics program called Microsoft® PowerPoint®.

Scientific visualization

Scientists use computer graphics programs to create images from scientific data. This process, known as visualization, helps scientists with their research. Chemists, for example, use programs called molecular modeling programs to build and study 3-D pictures or "models" of of the molecules that make up different substances.

Below are some 3-D models created with a program called WebLab ViewerPro.

A molecule of caffeine

A molecule of aspirin

A molecule of DNA

Graphics for games

3-D graphics are popular in computer games, because they make an imaginary situation more realistic and involving.

An aerial view of part of the race

These screen shots are taken from a racing game called Ultimate Race Pro™.

You can race against the computer or a friend...

... at different times of the day...

... and under different weather conditions.

Plans and designs

Many designers, from architects to landscape gardeners, use computers to produce 2-D and 3-D pictures of their ideas. This is known as Computer Aided Design (CAD). 3-D CAD permits designers to show other people, such as their customers, exactly what an object or place will look like when it is finished.

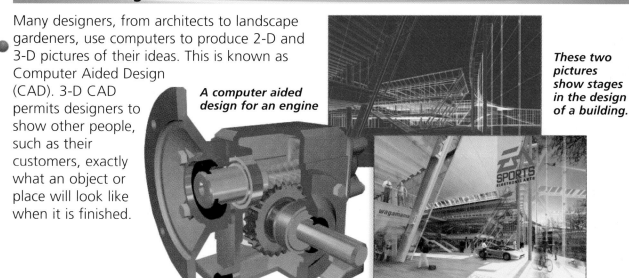

A computer aided design for an engine

These two pictures show stages in the design of a building.

3-D modeling

There are different types of software for producing 3-D models. For designing things that will be built, such as buildings or cars, 3-D designers use Computer Aided Design software.

For 3-D art, 3-D animations, graphics for computer games or multimedia CD-ROMs, designers use a type of software known as 3-D modeling software.

Modeling windows

3-D modeling software creates artificial 3-D spaces inside windows on a computer screen. Although the spaces are really only 2-D, they look and behave as though they are 3-D.

Most 3-D models are scenes made up of several parts or "objects". A designer models each object separately. When an object is ready, the designer positions it in a window called the scene window. Gradually, a scene is built up.

A 3-D modeling program called Ray Dream 3-D

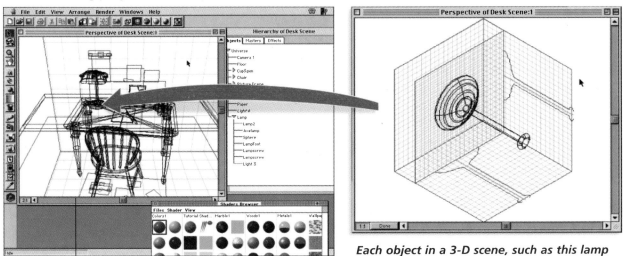

An artificial 3-D space called a scene window

Each object in a 3-D scene, such as this lamp base, is modeled in a separate window.

Planning

Before starting to recreate an object with modeling software, a designer collects and studies pictures, plans and real models of it. The designer breaks the object down into simple 3-D shapes. A hand, for example, could be broken down into spheres and cylinders as shown below.

The palm looks like a large flattened sphere.

Each finger is a cylinder.

Each joint looks like a small flattened sphere.

Wireframes

A designer starts building a 3-D object on a computer by constructing a 3-D frame known as a wireframe. This is a set of points joined by thin lines that represents the shape of the object. The object looks as though it is built out of bits of wire.

A computer can produce and manipulate wireframe objects more quickly than solid-looking objects.

A wireframe of a cow

3-D shapes

Basic 3-D shapes are known as primitives. Modeling software includes tools that a designer can use to create wireframes of primitives such as cubes, spheres, cylinders and ring shapes known as toruses.

A cube

A sphere

A torus

A cylinder

Primitives are like building blocks. A designer reshapes them or joins them together to produce other shapes.

This lollipop shape was created by joining a sphere and a cylinder.

Types of wireframe

Modeling programs include two methods for building wireframes: polygon modeling and spline-based modeling.

Polygon modeling means creating a wireframe out of many triangles and squares.

This wireframe of a desk lamp has been modeled with polygons.

Spline-based modeling means creating a wireframe out of curves.

Spline-based modeling creates a smooth surface so it is usually used for people and animals.

Specialist modeling software

Some modeling programs are specially designed to create particular types of models, such as figures or worlds. MetaCreations' Poser® 3, for example, is designed for creating human and animal figures.

A figure produced using Poser 3

You can obtain a free demonstration copy of some 3-D modeling programs including MetaCreations' Bryce® 3-D (see page 70). This is a world creation program which can create fantasy worlds.

A landscape produced using Bryce 3-D

Adding realism

After a wireframe model has been built, the next stage is to make it look solid and realistic. Before modeling software can do this, a 3-D designer must give it information about the object's appearance.

Covering a wireframe

Modeling software covers a wireframe with textures. There are usually a selection of ready-made textures to choose from, such as glass, wood and concrete.

A texture can be wrapped around any shape, including a sphere, as shown here.

Wood

Concrete

Glass

Each texture has different properties, such as color and shininess. These properties can be adjusted as required. For example, by making a wood texture appear to reflect objects in the scene, a designer can make it look as if the wood has been polished.

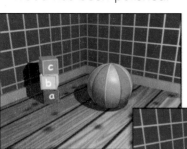

These two pictures show an ordinary wood texture (left) and a polished wood texture (below).

In this version, the toys are reflected in the floorboards, making the wood look more shiny.

Lighting a scene

To make a 3-D model look real and to give a scene an atmosphere, it is important to create the impression of light. The software must be given information about what kind of light, or lights, to use and where to position them around the model.

In modeling software, lights are represented by wireframe models which can be moved around the imaginary 3-D space.

There are two main kinds of lights: bulbs and spotlights. Bulbs illuminate a whole scene, and spotlights focus on a particular object or part of an object. The properties of these basic lights can be adjusted to create different effects, such as bright sunlight or flashlight. Adjustable properties include the brightness and color of a light and the length of its beams.

A wireframe of a bulb

This picture shows how light coming from a single bulb positioned above a scene can create the illusion of a bright, sunny day.

Bulb

The computer has worked out which areas of this scene should be in shadow.

Taking a picture

Next, the computer is instructed to draw a 2-D picture of one of the views of the model, using all the texture and lighting information that has been supplied. The process of drawing such a picture is called rendering.

To instruct the computer to render a model, the designer positions a wireframe model of a camera in the imaginary 3-D space. The computer draws what the camera would see. While deciding where to position the camera, a designer can move it around and look through it at the model or scene.

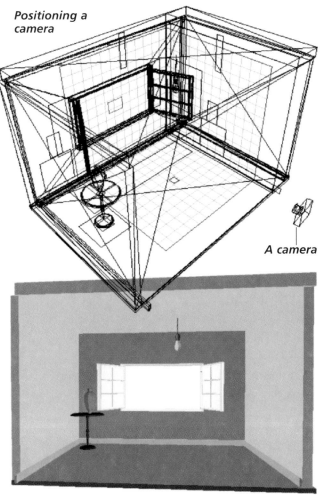

Positioning a camera

A camera

This is what the computer model looks like from the camera position shown above.

Rendering

There are different ways of rendering a 3-D model. To get a general idea of what a model looks like, a designer will choose a quick method of rendering. The image may look a bit rough, but it can be used to experiment with different surfaces, and check the lighting and the position of the camera.

This scene showing a lagoon was produced using a quick method of rendering.

A rendering method called ray tracing produces a high-quality result. It is very slow because it requires a computer to carry out millions of calculations. Ray tracing a scene may take several hours. Sometimes several computers are linked together to speed up the process.

A ray traced version of the scene shown above

Animating 3-D models

Animators can use 3-D modeling software to animate 3-D models. You can see 3-D computer animation in advertisements, computer games and movies.

These pictures show three different stages of modeling a creature from a 3-D animated television cartoon called Insektors.

The creature as it appears on TV

Creating key frames

To create a 3-D animation, an animator starts by building a wireframe model (see page 48) for each of the key frames (see page 37) of the animation. To produce a key frame for a 3-D animation, the animator positions a wireframe in a scene and sets a clock at a particular time. For example, for the first key frame of animation, the clock is set at 0 seconds. To produce the next key frame, the animator either moves the same model to a new position or changes the model's appearance or shape. The animator then sets the clock at a later time, such as 2 seconds.

Below are two key frames of an animation.

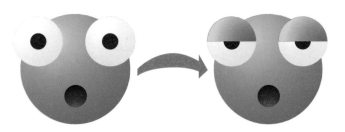

At 0 seconds the character's eyes are wide open.

At 2 seconds the character's eyes are beginning to close.

Model behavior

An animator can tell the computer precisely how a model should move. The way a model moves is known as its behavior. 3-D modeling programs include commands, known as tweeners, that let an animator make a model's behavior realistic. For example, when animating a racing car, the animator could use a tweener to make the car accelerate to its top speed and slow down after crossing the finishing line. If the car was animated without using a tweener, the car would start moving at top speed and stop instantly.

Frame rate

Finally, the animator tells the computer how many inbetween frames to produce per second of animation. Animated films and TV shows contain 24-30 frames per second, so that the animation appears smooth (see page 38). Animations for computer games, multimedia CD-ROMs and the World Wide Web usually contain only 15 frames per second, to keep the file as small as possible.

Once it has this information, a computer can start to render an animation.

Animating figures

One of the biggest problems in 3-D animation is making people and creatures move naturally. This can be solved using a technique called motion capture.

Motion capture is the process of collecting information about the way performers, such as actors or dancers, move. This information is fed into a computer and used to make 3-D models move realistically. The hardware and software used to collect the information is called a motion capture system.

This picture shows a magnetic motion capture system called Star Trak in action.

Capturing motion

There are two main types of motion capture systems: optical systems and magnetic systems. With optical systems, the actor or dancer wears markers that reflect light on important parts of their body, such as the head, knees and elbows. Several cameras capture the movement of the performer by recording the patterns of light that are reflected from the markers.

Magnetic systems, such as the one shown below, use magnetism instead of light. The performer moves inside a magnetic field, wearing magnetic sensors which capture movement.

This is a device called a transmitter. It produces a magnetic field in which a performer moves.

Magnetic sensors attached to the performer's body give out signals.

Electronic devices in a special motion capture suit turn the signals coming from the sensors into computer data.

The electronic devices can store computer data for up to 20 minutes of motion.

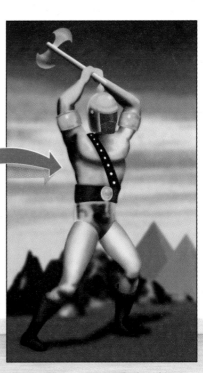

The movements made by the performer could be used to animate a 3-D character in a computer game.

Animated special effects

Many movies feature creatures that don't really exist. One way of producing these creatures is to use 3-D modeling and animation techniques. This is a big challenge for digital effects experts. The models must look real, as they will be combined with films of real people and places. However, producing realistic models is extremely difficult. Digital effects experts sometimes have to invent their own software to achieve the effects they require.

Computer creatures

One of the biggest challenges for digital effects experts is to create convincing computer-generated creatures. One of the first films to feature them was *Jurassic Park (1993)*. For this film, digital effects experts created 3-D animated models of dinosaurs. Although dinosaurs are extinct, people are familiar with similar creatures, such as lizards, and would notice if a digital representation of a dinosaur wasn't convincing.

For each dinosaur, digital effect experts first built and animated a wireframe. The wireframes were combined with filmed images of actors and scenery before the dinosaurs were given a skin texture.

Each frame of a computer animation is sharp whereas moving objects appear slightly blurred on film. Digital effects experts added blur to the dinosaurs to make their movements look more realistic.

Scenes from Jurassic Park

For this scene, the rain splashing onto the dinosaur was computer-generated.

A computer program made it look as if there were moving bones and muscles under the animal's skin.

The digital effects experts invented a program that allowed them to paint skin textures onto the wireframes instead of letting the modeling software apply the textures automatically. This gave them more control.

Artificial people

Computers are replacing people in many industries, including the movies. Computer animated actors or "synthespians" have already appeared in a number of films, including *The Borrowers (1997)*.

The Borrowers is about miniature people, called Borrowers, who live alongside humans.

Most of the time, the actors playing Borrowers were filmed in extra-large sets to make them look small. For some scenes, however, it was impossible to build big enough sets. Instead, animators created and animated small, digital versions of the actors. Then they combined these with film of a normal sized set.

Below are some pictures from the making of **The Borrowers.**

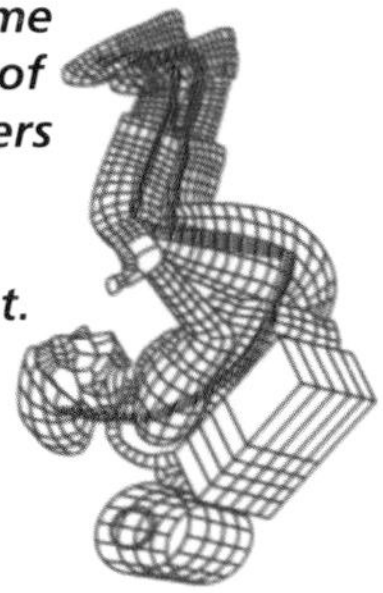

Information collected using motion capture was used to animate wireframe models of Borrowers like the one on the right.

A special scanner was used to scan an actor's head so that animators could give the model exactly the same features.

The computer-animated Borrower was combined with film images to produce the scene shown above.

For the scene shown below, computer animators created hundreds of synthespians.

This picture is the film image before the synthespians were added. It shows an actor playing a human tied up in a storeroom.

This is the final version of the scene after the synthespians were added. The human is now surrounded by a crowd of Borrowers.

Digital effects computers

3-D modeling for the movies requires a large amount of computer memory. Each frame of a film must be very detailed to look sharp and clear on a big screen. Computer-animated models for movies only started becoming possible in the 1980s when a company called

Silicon Graphics started making computers called Silicon Graphics workstations. These are designed for processing picture information quickly. Even with specially designed equipment, it can still take several hours to render a single frame of a realistic 3-D animation.

Computer environments

From indoor studios to the open air, computer graphics are replacing real scenery, sets and background paintings in both film and television.

Virtual TV studios

When TV presenters appear to be sitting in spacious, well-decorated studios, they may only be sitting in front of a blue screen. A computer-generated background, known as a virtual studio, is added to the television images before or as they are broadcast. The word "virtual" means something that isn't real, but is a computer version of something real.

Virtual studio

The picture above shows the image the TV camera shoots.

The picture on the right shows the image that is broadcast.

Simulating scenery

Realistic computer animation can be used to reproduce scenery that moves or changes shape, such as water, fire, rain and other types of weather.

Computer-generated scenery is particularly useful for films which feature events that are difficult or dangerous to film, such as volcano eruptions, lightning or tornadoes.

Below are two pictures from the making of a film called Cheese (1998).

This picture shows a shot of a village filmed from a distance.

This picture shows the shot above after computer graphics software was used to simulate a twilight sky, drifting clouds and a ball of lightning shooting upwards.

Mathematical pictures

Some of the most unusual and intricate computer graphics are known as fractals. They are produced from mathematical equations. When the letters in an equation are replaced by certain numbers, a computer interprets them as curves and points in a picture.

Some of the patterns in fractals resemble things in nature, such as leaves.

A selection of fractals

Fractals can be used to create natural looking textures for computer art. Some of the textures in this landscape were produced using fractals.

Fractals are usually abstract patterns.

Repeating patterns

If you look closely at one of the fractals above, you will see big and small versions of the same patterns. Parts of the patterns in a fractal repeat themselves again and again, no matter how much you magnify it.

If you have access to the Internet, you can try magnifying a fractal using a program on the World Wide Web. It is at this Web address: http://home.rmi.net/~tph/fractalkit/fractal.html.

A fractal

A close-up of the same fractal

Create a fractal

You don't need to understand the complicated mathematics involved to create your own beautiful fractals. You can use a computer program called Test Fractal Generator. This program is on the World Wide Web at this Web address: http://zenith.berkeley.edu/seidel/Frac/.

Test Fractal Generator allows you to alter numbers in a mathematical equation that produces a fractal. To do this, you type numbers into the boxes on the Web page. When you have done this, select the dimensions of your fractal from the list labeled *Size of x,y fields in pixels*. Finally, click on the *Crank it up* button to see the fractal produced by your numbers. If the numbers you choose don't produce an interesting image, try with other numbers to see what effect they have.

Graphics for games

Racing a car, flying a plane, fighting an enemy, solving a mystery or ruling a civilization - these are just a few of the imaginary situations computer games can allow you to enjoy. Computer graphics play an important role in making the experience entertaining and exciting.

Improving graphics

The graphics used in games are continually getting more detailed, and many games now have spectacular 3-D graphics. This is because home computers are becoming more powerful and can process picture data more and more quickly. They can now display more realistic graphics, while ensuring that the action on screen takes place in "real-time". This means the graphics change instantly in response to a player's instructions.

Games on TV

Some computers, known as consoles, are designed specifically for playing games. When you connect a console to a television set, it displays graphics on the screen.

All computers contain electronic devices, known as chips, that process computer data. Consoles contain chips that specialize in processing 3-D graphics data.

This console is called a Nintendo 64.

There is no keyboard or mouse. Instead, you use this device, called a joypad, to control the computer.

A screen shot from a 2-D game called Mario Bros.

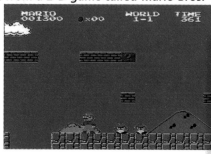

Early games, like this one, had very simple graphics that only contained a few colors.

A screen shot from a more recent 2-D game called Mario AllStars

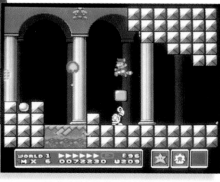

The graphics from this game contain more detail and a greater variety of colors.

These 3-D graphics from games called Super Mario 64 and Mario Kart 64 are vivid and realistic.

Two types of graphics

Some computer games contain two different types of graphics. Some are "interactive". This means that they change according to your actions. Others are "non-interactive", which means that you can't change them.

You usually see non-interactive graphics in animation or video sequences that introduce different stages of the game. The graphics for these sequences are produced in advance.

You see interactive graphics as you play a game. Using a device such as a keyboard, mouse, joystick, joypad, or driving wheel, you give the game information about the actions you want to take. A piece of software called a game engine uses this information to work out what graphics to display on screen. The game engine animates the characters and changes the scenery of a game in real-time.

A driving wheel

The above picture shows non-interactive graphics from the introductory sequence to a game called Rascal. The boy's face, arms and T-shirt are smooth and rounded.

This picture shows interactive 3-D graphics from Rascal. Notice how the boy's arms and T-shirt look as if they are made out of blocks.

Adding reality

Companies that make computer games use a number of different techniques to make the scenery and action more realistic. For example, they use data collected by motion capture systems (see page 53) to animate fighting characters in action games. For sports games, settings such as race tracks and golf courses are based on real locations.

The landscapes for this flying game called Flight Unlimited II were produced from aerial photographs.

Altitude: 667 ft   Airspeed: 117 kts   Heading: 173

3-D computer graphics play a vital part in "Virtual Reality" (VR). This is the use of computers to create artificial places which appear to be real. These places are known as virtual worlds.

You can explore a virtual world freely, going where you like, when you like, and picking up and moving the objects that you come across. As you do so, you can see, hear, and sometimes feel and even smell, your surroundings.

Inside a virtual world

The graphics in virtual worlds are real-time and interactive (see pages 58-59). They change instantly according to your actions. For example, as you approach an object in a virtual world, it appears to get bigger.

As you explore a virtual world, the computer that is creating the world has to draw new graphics continually. Different methods are used to enable the computer to draw the graphics quickly enough. One of these involves reducing the level of detail of objects that are in the distance, as shown below.

A screen shot from a Virtual Reality office

The items on the desk are drawn as simple blocks.

When you look at the telephone close up, the computer redraws it in more detail.

Immersive VR

There are two main types of Virtual Reality: immersive VR and desktop VR (see page 61). Immersive VR makes you feel as though you are actually inside a virtual world. You need to use special VR equipment to experience this.

Some immersive VR systems consist of a helmet called a head-mounted display (HMD), a hand-held control device, and a tracking system. A tracking system is a device that senses the movements you make and reports them to the computer that is creating the virtual world. With other immersive VR systems, you stand or sit in an enclosed space, such as a room or sphere and look at computer graphics displayed on the walls.

A virtual supermarket

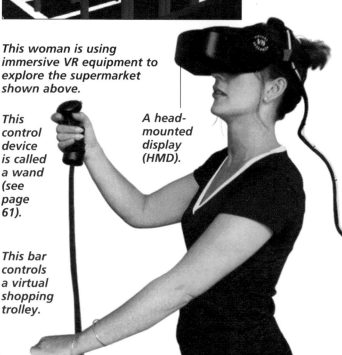

This woman is using immersive VR equipment to explore the supermarket shown above.

This control device is called a wand (see page 61).

A head-mounted display (HMD).

This bar controls a virtual shopping trolley.

Head-mounted displays

Because there is a distance between your eyes, each eye sees a slightly different image of your surroundings. Your brain combines these images to obtain information about depth and distance.

A head-mounted display enables you to see a virtual world in the same way that you see the real world. Most include a small screen and a set of special lenses for each eye. Each screen shows a slightly different view of the virtual world. When you look at both screens at the same time, you see a single 3-D picture which seems to be very realistic. An HMD, which uses two screens in this way, is called stereoscopic.

A head-mounted display

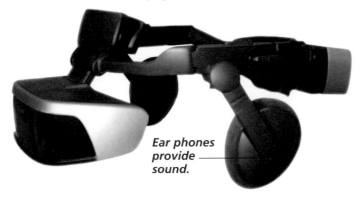

Ear phones provide sound.

Control devices

There are two main types of hand-held control devices for immersive VR: wands and instrumented gloves. You can use either of them to indicate to the computer that you are moving or grasping a virtual object. Some instrumented gloves can make you feel as though you are touching objects in the virtual world.

A wand

You can use the buttons to give the computer information about where you want to go or what you want to do.

An instrumented glove

Devices attached to an instrumented glove collect information about the movement of the hand inside the glove, and send this information to the computer.

Desktop VR

For desktop VR, you only need a desktop computer. You look at the computer graphics on the computer's monitor. As a result, you feel as though you are looking at a virtual world from outside. To move around the world, you use a hand-held control such as a mouse or joystick.

Some desktop VR systems include stereoscopic glasses and a joystick that allows you to feel the things you touch.

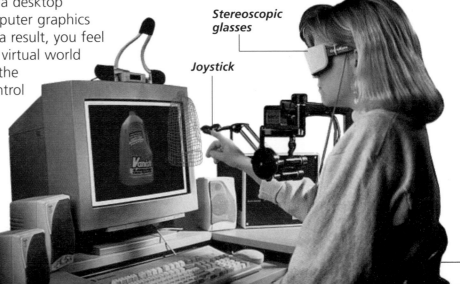

Stereoscopic glasses

Joystick

Using Virtual Reality

Virtual Reality can be used to create reconstructions of things which exist in the real world, or completely imaginary environments which you can explore for fun. Reconstructions of real places are most often used in business, industry and education for specific purposes such as planning or training.

Digital designs

Designers of large structures, such as ships and supermarkets, use Virtual Reality to perfect their plans. By turning their ideas into virtual worlds, they can ensure the structures match all the necessary requirements and foresee any possible problems before they are built.

The two pictures below show a Virtual Reality chemical factory.

This is the interior of one of the floors of the factory.

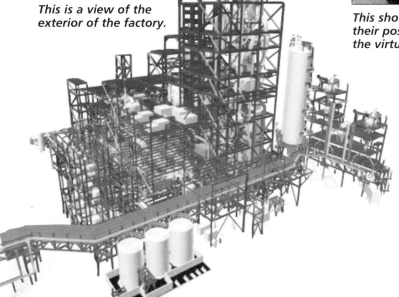

This is a view of the exterior of the factory.

Education

Virtual Reality can be included in educational software to make lessons more enjoyable and memorable. For example, the program shown below teaches children how to become responsible citizens and how to prevent crime. Users explore a virtual city, taking on different roles, such as police officer or witness. When they discover crimes, they have to decide what action to take, and then face up to the consequences of their decisions.

The pictures below are screen shots from a program called **Crime Conquest.**

The scene of a crime in a virtual school - a schoolroom which was set on fire by criminals

This shows users their position in the virtual school.

The scene of a real crime - a photograph of a schoolroom that was destroyed by fire

A view of the destroyed schoolroom

Training

Virtual Reality is used to train people, such as pilots and doctors, to perform tasks such as flying a plane or performing an operation. They can practice their jobs and make mistakes without damaging anything or hurting anyone.

A flight simulator is used for training pilots. It is a real cockpit mounted on a moving platform.

Inside, a trainee pilot flies between cities in a virtual world.

The controls are real. *Computer screens show computer graphics that resemble reality.*

Engineers can use the virtual world below to learn how to maintain a jet engine.

Virtual history

You can travel back through time by exploring a Virtual Reality reconstruction of a historical site. Some reconstructions show sites as they would have been when they were in perfect condition. These enable people to visit temples and palaces that no longer exist. Other reconstructions show sites in their current state.

Below is a VR reconstruction of the inside of an ancient temple at Gebel Barkal, in Sudan, Africa.

© 1998 Learning Sites, Inc.

This reconstruction is based on archaeological discoveries.

Below is a VR reconstruction of a prehistoric stone circle called Stonehenge, in Wiltshire, UK.

The virtual world is an accurate record of the site in its current state.

This close-up of some virtual stones shows how much detail there is in the virtual world.

Using graphics in medicine

Computer graphics are used in medicine to allow doctors to see inside people's bodies without cutting them open. This is known as medical imaging.

Scanning humans

Pictures of the inside of a human body are produced using medical scanners. Different types of scanners use different methods to obtain pictures. Important methods used in medical imaging include X-ray Computed Tomography (X-ray CT), Magnetic Resonance Imaging (MRI), and Nuclear Medicine imaging.

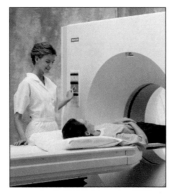

This scanner produces X-ray CT images.

The patient lies on a bed which slides into the scanner.

Adding color

A computer can change the colors of an image produced by a scanner. This makes it easier for doctors to interpret the information in the images. For example, the computer could be instructed to color parts of the brain according to how they react to something.

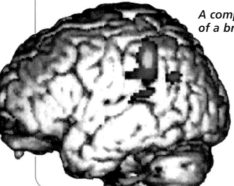

A computer image of a brain

The colored area became more active when water was squirted into the patient's ear.

X-ray CT

Tomography is a process in which photographs of cross-sections, or "slices", of a solid object are obtained. X-ray Computed Tomography is carried out by a CT scanner. X-rays are passed through the body, then a computer converts the information that they collect into a picture.

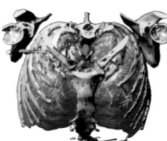

X-ray CT is also known as Computerized Axial Tomography (CAT).

This picture of a pair of lungs was created from images produced by a CAT scanner.

MRI

Magnetic Resonance Imaging is produced by placing a patient in a very strong magnetic field inside a machine called an MR scanner. An MR scanner records the way water molecules inside the body react to the magnetic field. It then feeds the results into a computer, which creates an image.
   Magnetic Resonance Imaging is usually used for looking at parts of the body such as muscles, brain and spinal cord.

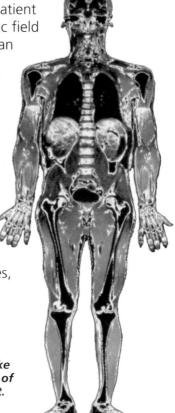

An MRI image of a woman. Color has been added to make the different parts of the body stand out.

Nuclear Medicine Imaging

There are two types of Nuclear Medicine Imaging: Positron Emission Tomography (PET) and Single Photo Emission Computed Tomography (SPECT). Both require a patient to drink a liquid or receive an injection containing some very slightly radioactive chemicals. These chemicals are absorbed by the body and send out faint radiation signals. The signals are detected either by a scanner (PET) or by a device called a gamma camera (SPECT). They are then turned into images by a computer.

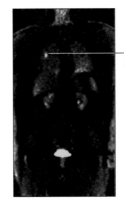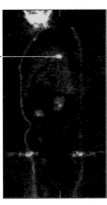

Two PET scans of the same patient taken from different angles. The small yellow dot is a suspected lung tumour.

3-D images

The pictures obtained by the methods described on these pages can be used to produce 3-D images of the structures inside the body. Images are obtained from various angles and fed into a computer. The computer combines the information contained in the images to produce a 3-D model. 3-D models are used to discover medical problems and to plan surgical operations.

Guiding surgeons

3-D images can also be used to help surgeons during operations. Before an operation, a computer produces a model of the part of the body that requires surgery. During the operation, the computer tracks the position of the surgeon's instruments. It uses the model to indicate their exact location. This information enables a surgeon to work more quickly and accurately. This technique, known as image-guided surgery, is most often used during brain operations.

A screen shot from an image-guided surgery program showing a 3-D model of a brain

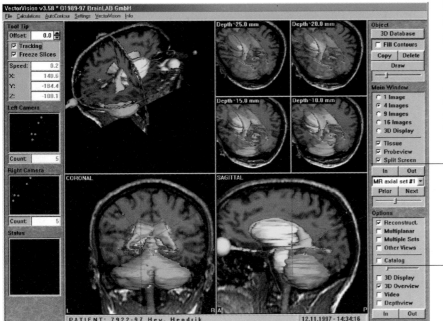

The surgeon can view the model from several angles at once.

Displaying graphics

A computer shows pictures on a screen. To do this, it requires two pieces of equipment: a graphics card and a monitor. These two devices work together to produce a screen image from information that the computer provides.

From pulses to pictures

A computer produces a description of the letters, numbers and pictures that make up a screen image. The information is in the form of electronic pulses, known as digital signals. The computer sends the digital signals to a graphics card. This converts the digital signals into electrical waves, known as analog signals, then passes them onto the monitor. A monitor can only produce pictures from analog signals.

A graphics card

A graphics card fits inside the computer.

About monitors

Most computer monitors are large plastic boxes that look like TV sets. These monitors are called cathode ray tube (CRT) monitors, because they contain a device called a cathode ray tube. This turns the analog signals coming from the graphics card into a screen image.

A CRT monitor

Screen

Close-up of a screen

A screen is divided into a grid of hundreds of thousands of small dots. These dots are called picture elements, or pixels. A monitor produces an image on screen by making the pixels glow different colors.

A computer monitor

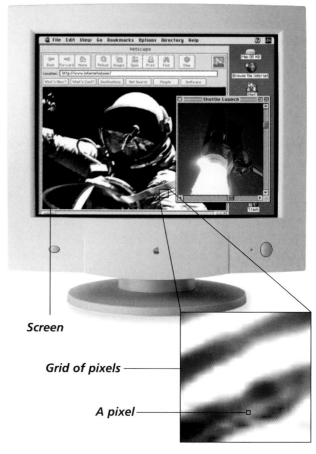

Screen

Grid of pixels

A pixel

Screen pixels

Each pixel on a monitor's screen is made up of three tiny colored dots of chemicals called phosphors. Phosphors glow when tiny particles called electrons touch them.

A pixel is a group of three dots of phosphor: a red one, a green one and a blue one.

Inside a monitor

At the back of a monitor, there is a cathode ray tube. It contains three electron guns. Each electron gun shoots a beam of electrons down the tube at the screen.

One beam of electrons hits only the red phosphor dots in each pixel, another hits the green dots and the third hits the blue dots. The beams are directed to the correct dots by a thin sheet of metal with holes in it. This is called a shadow mask.

Glowing pixels

Signals produced by a graphics card control the strength of each beam when it hits a particular dot of phosphor. The stronger the beam, the brighter the dot glows.

The three dots of phosphor in a pixel are so small that the pixel appears to be glowing only one color. Different colored pixels are produced by variations in how brightly the three dots of phosphor glow. By making the pixels glow different colors, a monitor produces an image on screen.

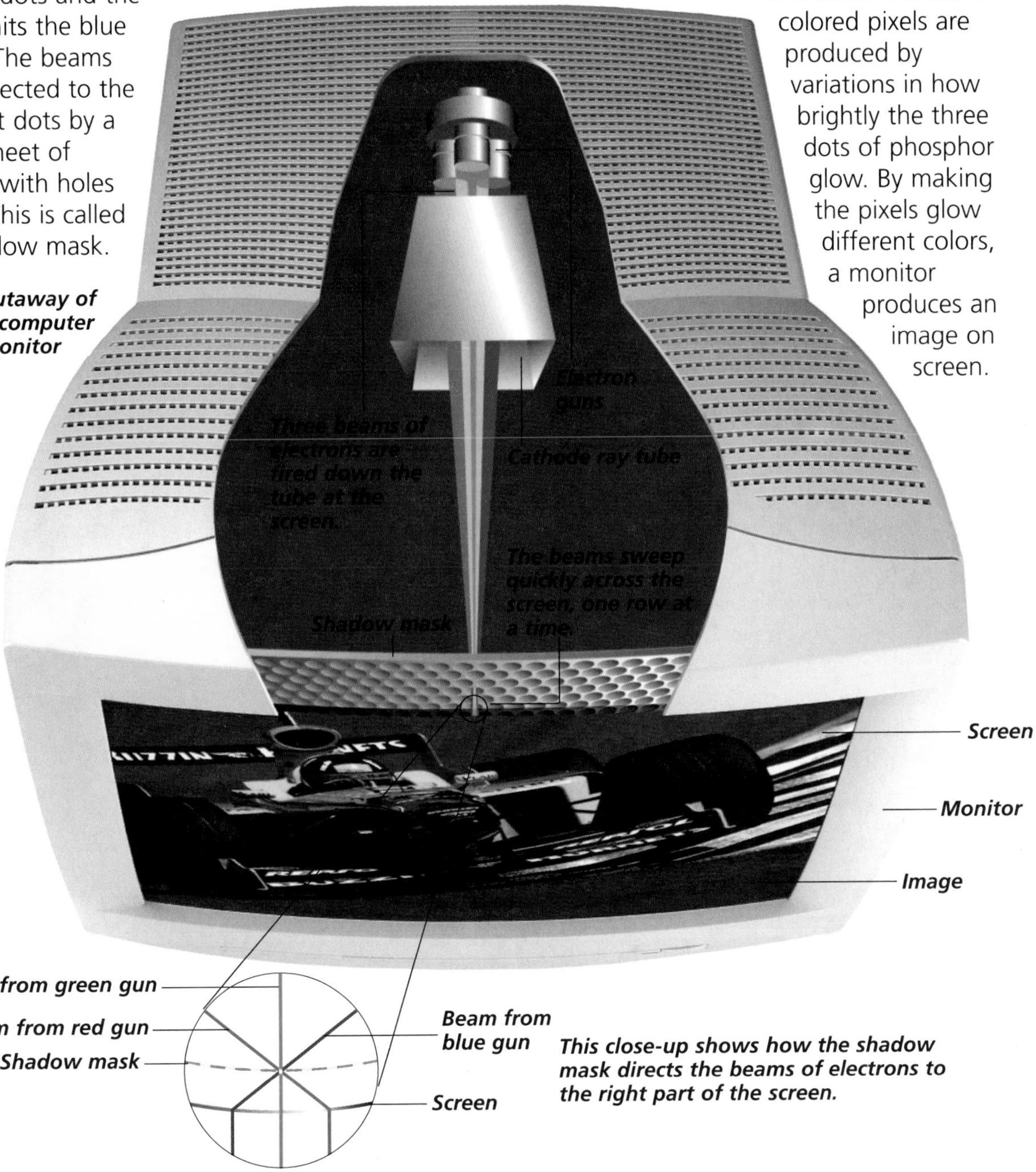

Cutaway of a computer monitor

Three beams of electrons are fired down the tube at the screen.

Electron guns

Cathode ray tube

The beams sweep quickly across the screen, one row at a time.

Shadow mask

Screen

Monitor

Image

Beam from green gun

Beam from red gun

Shadow mask

Beam from blue gun

Screen

This close-up shows how the shadow mask directs the beams of electrons to the right part of the screen.

67

Computer graphics look clearer and more colorful on some screens than on others. The quality of a screen image depends on its "color depth" and resolution. Color depth is the maximum number of different colors the image can contain. Resolution is the number of pixels into which the screen is divided.

Color depth

The number of different colors a monitor can display depends on the graphics card that controls it. Most computers contain 16-bit graphics cards. This means the monitor can show up to 64,000 different colors.

You can instruct a monitor to show a different number of colors, providing this is less than the maximum number the graphics card can process. For example, a monitor controlled by a 16-bit graphics card can also be set to show 16 or 256 different colors. (Find out how on page 69.) An image looks better when it is displayed on a screen set at 64,000 colors than when it is displayed on a screen set at 256 colors.

This picture shows two different colour depths.

16 colors   **64,000 colors**

Resolution

Screen resolution measures how many pixels a screen is divided into. For example, a screen which is divided into a grid that is 640 pixels across and 480 pixels down is said to have a resolution of 640 x 480.

A screen can have different resolutions, as long as the graphics card that controls it has enough memory to store the total number of pixels required. (Find out how to change a screen's resolution on page 69.)

These pictures show the same screen set at two different resolutions.

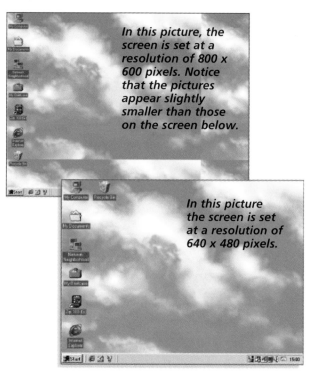

In this picture, the screen is set at a resolution of 800 x 600 pixels. Notice that the pictures appear slightly smaller than those on the screen below.

In this picture the screen is set at a resolution of 640 x 480 pixels.

Pixel size

The resolution of a screen affects the size of the pixels. A screen set at a resolution of 1280 x 1024 contains many more pixels than a screen set at a resolution of 640 x 480. This means that each individual pixel is much smaller in the higher resolution screen.

⚠️ The instructions on this page explain how to change the way a computer controlled by the Windows® 95 or 98 operating system displays graphics. Before you follow these instructions, close any programs that are open on your computer.

Display properties

To control your computer's display, you need to use the Settings sheet in the Display Properties dialog box. To find this dialog box, select _Settings_ from the Start menu. From the menu which appears, select _Control Panel_. In the Control Panel window, double-click on the Display icon and the Display Properties dialog box will open. Click on the _Settings_ tab to bring the Settings sheet to the front.

The Display icon

Part of the Display Properties dialog box is shown below.

Changing color depth

To change the color depth of your display, use the drop-down list called _Color palette_ or _Colors_. Click on the arrow to see a list of the color depths that your computer can display, such as 256 Color and 16 Color. Select an option from the list and click _OK_.

The Color palette control

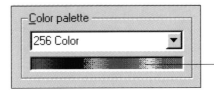

This color spectrum changes when you select a different option from the list.

A message will appear on your screen asking you whether or not you want to restart your computer right away. Choose the option that instructs your computer to restart. Your computer will use the new color setting when it starts up again.

Changing screen resolution

To change the resolution of your screen (see page 68), use the slider bar called _Desktop area_ or _Screen area_, then click _Apply_ followed by _OK_.

The Desktop area slider bar

Drag the bar to the left to decrease the number of pixels into which your screen is divided.

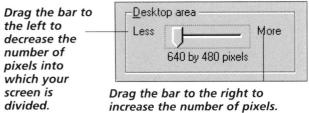

Drag the bar to the right to increase the number of pixels.

Your screen will flicker or go black for a while, then you will see what your chosen resolution looks like. At the same time, a message will appear. This asks whether you want to keep the new resolution. If you do, click _Yes_. If you click _No_ or don't do anything, your computer will return to the original resolution after a few seconds.

You can obtain graphics software from stores and by mail order. You will find information about companies that sell software by mail order in computer magazines.

Some computer magazines have a CD-ROM attached to the cover. Look out for trial copies of graphics programs on magazine cover discs.

If you have Internet access, you will be able to obtain both trial copies and full copies of many programs from the Web sites of the companies that make them. If a program is not available on the company's Web site, look around for information about how to obtain the program elsewhere.

If you have trouble finding a particular program, use the information below to contact the company that makes it. They will be able to tell you how to obtain their programs.

Wherever possible, the information below includes addresses, e-mail addresses and Web site addresses.

Programs mentioned in this book

p16 **Adobe® Illustrator®**: Adobe Systems Inc., 345 Park Avenue, San Jose, CA 95110-2704, USA
http://www.adobe.com/
CorelDRAW™: Corel Corporation, 1600 Carling Avenue, Ottowa, Ontario, Canada, K1Z 8R7
http://www.corel.com/
Macromedia Freehand: Macromedia Inc., 600 Townsend Street, San Francisco, CA 94103, USA
http://www.macromedia.com/
Mayura Draw: Mayura Software, P.O. Box 50158, Palo Alto, CA 94303, USA
http://www.mayura.com/
p24 **Adobe® Photoshop®**: (as Adobe Illustrator)
Paint Shop Pro: JASC Software Inc., Attn: Sales Dept., P.O. Box 44997, Eden Prairie, MN 55343, USA

http://www.jasc.com/
p29 **Kai's Power Tools**: MetaCreations, Attn: Sales Department, 6303 Carpinteria Avenue, Carpinteria, CA 93013, USA
E-mail: intlsales@metacreations.com
http://www.metacreations.com/
Adobe® Gallery Effects®: (as Adobe Illustrator)
p35 **PKZIP®**: Sales Group, PKWARE Inc., 9025 N. Deerwood Drive, Brown Deer, WI 53223, USA
E-mail: sales@pkware.com
http://www.pkware.com/
WinZip: Nico Mak Computing Inc., P.O. Box 540, Mansfield, CT 06268, USA
http://www.winzip.com/
StuffIt: Aladdin Systems Inc., 165 Westridge Drive, Watsonville, CA 95076, USA
E-mail: intl@aladdinsys.com
http://www.aladdinsys.com/
p38 **GIF Animator**: Ulead Systems Inc., 10F, No. 45 Tung Hsing Road, Taipei, Taiwan, Republic of China
http://www.ulead.com/
p41 **MorphMan**: Stoik Software
http://www.stoik.com/
p42 **Adobe® Premiere®**: (as Adobe Illustrator)

Alternative programs

p4-5 A basic painting program for Macs is included with **Appleworks®**: Apple Computer Inc., 1 Infinite Loop, M/S 303-4PR, Cupertino, CA 95014, USA
http://www.apple.com/appleworks/
p24 **Adobe® PhotoDeluxe™**: (as Adobe Illustrator)
p29 **Paint Alchemy**: Xaos Tools Inc., 433 California St., Ninth Floor, San Francisco, CA 94104-1905, USA
http://www.xaostools.com/
p40 **Morph™**: Gryphon Software
Fax: +1 425 562 4223
http://gryphonsw.com/morph/index.html

Index

Every effort has been made to trace the copyright holders of the material in this book. If any rights have been omitted, the publishers offer their sincere apologies and will rectify this in any subsequent editions, following notification.

Microsoft and Microsoft Windows are registered trademarks of Microsoft Corporation in the United States and other countries. Screen shots and icons reprinted with permission from Microsoft Corporation.

Cover: Hand. ©Telegraph Colour Library. Dice and spaceship. ©The Stock Market Photo Agency (UK). Adobe and Photoshop are trademarks of Adobe Systems Incorporated.
Cover (and p1 and 52): Insektors. ©Fantôme. Used with permission.
Cover (and p37): Inbetweening graphics. Copyright ©Cambridge Animation Systems.
p2 (and p47): CAD of building. Courtesy of Electronic Arts Ltd and Foster and Partners, Architects. Visualization by Foster Visualization.
p3: Fractal. ©Alfred Pasieke/Science Photo Library. Weather map. ©NASA/Science Photo Library. Dragon Heart. The Moviestore Collection.
p18: Adobe and Illustrator are trademarks of Adobe Systems Incorporated.
p19: Graphics tablet. ©1998 Wacom Technology Corporation.
p20: Scanners. With thanks to Lincoln Bealsey PR and Storm Technology for loan of the PageScan USB sheet-fed scanner and the TotalScan Express flatbed scanner.
p21: Scanner diagram based on a diagram from "An Introduction to Digital Scanning" by kind permission of Agfa-Gevaert.
Digital camera. The Agfa ePhoto 1280, a part of Agfa's award winning range of digital cameras and desktop scanners.
p21 (and p66): PowerMac G3 computer and monitor. Photography courtesy of Apple Computer (UK) Ltd.
p22: Scanning software. Courtesy of Epson (UK) Ltd.
p22 (and p23): Women. Dolding/Tony Stone Images.
p24: Paint Shop Pro. Courtesy of Kris Tufto, CEO, Jasc Software, Inc. Snowboarder. Jeff Stock/Tony Stone Images. Motorcyclist. Don Johnston/Tony Stone Images.
p25: Skateboarder. Joe McBride/Tony Stone Images.
p27: Skyline. Demetrio Carrasco/Tony Stone Images. Fish. ©Telegraph Colour Library. Zebra. Purdy Matt-Lamberti/Tony Stone Images.
p30: Hewlett-Packard Laserjet 6L printer. Courtesy of Hewlett-Packard. Epson Stylus Colour 800 printer. Courtesy of Epson (UK) Ltd.
p31: Hewlett-Packard printer software. Courtesy of Hewlett-Packard.
p32: Tiger. Tim Davies/Tony Stone Images.
p33: iMac. Photography courtesy of Apple Computer (UK) Ltd.
p34: Information kiosk. Crown Copyright. Photograph courtesy of UK Central Computer and Telecommunications Agency.
Web page. Courtesy of NASA.
Multimedia CD-ROM. Copyright ©Usborne Publishing and Great Bear Technology.
p36: "Smartipants" commercial. Reproduced by kind permission of Nestlé SA. Courtesy of JWT on behalf of Nestlé/Rowntree. With thanks to Aardman animations.
Flying Toasters screen saver. Berkeley Systems, a division of Sierra.
Puzzle Castle multimedia CD-ROM. Copyright ©Media Station.
"MUNGIE". Courtesy of Cosgrove Hall Films.
Animated mouse pointers. Eileen Fitzgibbons is a Flight Attendant who lives in Orlando, Florida, USA.
Jazz JackRabbit. Courtesy of Epic MegaGames.
p37: Storyboard. Rolie Polie Olie Series. ©1998 Nelvana Limited. Finished image. ©1998 Nelvana Limited/Métal Hurlant Productions s.a.r.l. All rights reserved.
p38 (and p39): Ulead GIF Animator 2.0. Courtesy of Ulead Systems, Inc.
p40: Willow. COURTESY OF LUCASFILM LTD.
Black or White. Copyright ©MJJ Productions, Inc.
p42: Rainbow Runner video capture card. Courtesy of Matrox Graphics, Inc.

Digital video camera. Artwork supplied by Panasonic UK Ltd.
Adobe and Adobe Premiere are trademarks of Adobe Systems Incorporated.
p44: Braveheart. The Computer Film Company. http://www.cfc.co.uk. Men in Black. The Moviestore Collection.
p46: Molecular graphics courtesy of Molecular Simulations Inc., Cambridge, UK.
p47: Ultim@te Race Pro. ©1996/1998 Kalisto Technologies. All rights reserved. Ultim@te Race Pro and Kalisto Entertainment are trademarks of Kalisto Technologies. Published by MicroProse. MicroProse is a registered trademark of MicroProse Ltd.
Engine designed in AutoCAD. Picture courtesy of Autodesk.
p48: Ray Dream 3-D. Courtesy of MetaCreations Corporation.
p49: Sample Art produced in Bryce 3D and Poser 3. Courtesy of MetaCreations Corporation.
p53: Star Trak. Courtesy of Polhemus Incorporated - 1998.
p54: Jurassic Park. The Moviestore Collection.
p55: The Borrowers. Polygram/Pictorial Press. Digital FX created by Digital Film @ The Moving Picture Co., London.
p56: Virtual TV studio. By courtesy of BBC Resources Ltd's unique Virtual Studio. Cheese. Images courtesy of P. Gilbert, Director.
p57: Fractal images by Paul Carlson. pjcarlsn@ix.netcom.com
Fractal landscape. ©Gregory Sams/Science Photo Library.
p58: Nintendo 64 console and screen shots from Mario games. Courtesy of THE Games.
p59: Rascal. ©1990-8 Psygnosis Limited. Used with permission. All rights reserved. Flight Unlimited II. ©Intermetrics Entertainment LLC and Looking Glass Studios 1998. Flight Unlimited is a registered trademark of Intermetrics Entertainment LLC and Looking Glass Studios.
p60:. VR office. ©Superscape. +44 (0)1256 745745. VR supermarket and immersive VR equipment. Courtesy of Virtual Presence Ltd.
p61: Sony Glasstron HMD. Courtesy of Sony United Kingdom Limited. Immersive VR wand. Courtesy of Virtual Presence Ltd. Created using handgrip from TOP GUN® Joystick by Thrustmaster. TOP GUN ™ & ©1996 Paramount Pictures. All Rights Reserved. TOP GUN is a trademark of Paramount Pictures. Instrumented glove. Courtesy of Virtual Presence Ltd and Virtual Technologies, Inc. Desktop VR. Courtesy of Virtual Presence Ltd and Sensable Technologies, Inc.
p62: Chemical plant and Crime Conquest. Courtesy of Virtual Presence Ltd.
p63: Stonehenge and jet engine. Courtesy of Virtual Presence Ltd.
Flight simulator exterior and interior. Photographs courtesy of Thomson Training & Simulation. Gebel Barkal. Copyright ©1998 by Learning Sites, Inc. http://www.learningsites.com. Reprinted by permission.
p64: Somatom +4 CT scanner. Image with kind permission of Siemens Medical Engineering.
Brain. By courtesy of the Department of Biomedical Physics, University of Aberdeen. Lungs. ©Volker Sieger/Siemens/Science Photo Library.
Body. ©J.C. Revy/Science Photo Library.
p65: PET scans. By courtesy of the Department of Biomedical Physics, University of Aberdeen. VectorVision image-guided surgery system. Image courtesy of BrainLAB, Germany.
p66: Graphics Card. Viper V330 2D and 3D Graphics Accelerator. Diamond Multimedia Systems Ltd.
p67: Screen image. Courtesy of Jordan Grand Prix.
p68: First Mission to Earth artwork. Courtesy of Keith Scaife, Sarah Brown Agency.

First published in America in 1999 by Usborne Publishing Ltd, Usborne House, 83-85 Saffron Hill, London, EC1N 8RT, England. www.usborne.com. Copyright ©1999 Usborne Publishing Ltd. The name Usborne and the device 🐝 are Trade Marks of Usborne Publishing Ltd. All rights reserved. No part of this publication may be reproduced, stored in a retrieval system or transmitted in any form, or by any means, electronic, mechanical, photocopying, recording or otherwise, without the prior permission of the publisher. AE. Printed in Spain.